GO

The Rev. John ... ...
priest of the Ch ... ...
served parishes ... ...
over the years 1963–1973. In that year he
became Chaplain to the Ryhope Hospitals in
Sunderland. Since 1983 he has been Chaplain
to Hill End Hospital, St Albans.

Mr Woolley is the author of several books,
including *I Am With You* and *God's
Opportunities*, which are also published by
Fount.

For
Edna, Sally,
Liz and Peter

GOD'S PROMISES

John Woolley

Collins
FOUNT PAPERBACKS

First published in Great Britain in 1987,
by Fount Paperbacks, London

Copyright © John Woolley 1987

Made and printed in Great Britain by
William Collins Sons & Co. Ltd, Glasgow

Contents

Introduction

Really warm experiences of God are few and far between . . . for most people!

I'm sure that this lack of warmth is one of the reasons why
so many Christians become resigned to their situation, and
settle, instead, for stoical "Church activity", or perhaps
endless discussion, reports and "re-thinking". Not to
mention (said he apologetically) . . . endless writing!

In the midst of all this often-frustrating religious
effort, we can forget that there exist some wonderful
promises from God . . . promises which we can make
personal, and use to revolutionize our lives.

These promises, as we build them into our lives, are
able to bring an exciting sense of reality into our relationship with God.

* * *

Changed Reactions

We know that God doesn't exactly overwhelm most of us
with a sense of His presence! But God *has* given to so
many people, through the centuries, very clear
statements about His intentions, some very clear and
loving promises.

We can either take these statements seriously . . . or we can treat them as historical curiosities for theologians to argue about.

The promises which we find in the Bible are not just nice-sounding thoughts cooked up by some old priest in around 400 B.C. Those promises are God-given, dynamic, and ready to transform our present situation, whatever it is. We just need to take a firm grip on some of those promises, and find that they are a marvellous way of realizing our ambition to live close to God.

We may be full of guilt, full of fears (both "normal" and irrational); we may be involved in unsatisfactory relationships, or in terribly discouraging circumstances; we may even feel like giving up altogether.

Well, those promises of God are just waiting there . . . to help us to make a sharp turn-around in our reactions.

As we get hold of those promises, and make them part of our life, we can expect a sense of God's love, and of His work on our behalf, to become much stronger.

*   *   *

It's terribly sad that most "believers" grasp only a little of what God is offering. . . .

Just as God can, so to speak, come out of a printed page and start to live in someone, so, too, can a promise (which, previously, we've merely "read"), become part of us.

We may even find that we can now quote some of those promises to our surprised Christian friends!

Those who believe in God can't escape for long the impact of many uncomfortable facts, many harsh realities of existence. What God's promises do, once we start

8

really to live by them, is to give us an amazing new *perspective* about those hard facts.

It's doubtful whether any other recorded words have had such a drastic effect on so many lives. . . .

Taking a good look at God's promises and living by them isn't meant to be an optional extra for people who believe in Him. . . . God meant those promises to be *absolutely central* to our lives.

Those promises are there to motivate us in all sorts of ways. . . .

. . . .Which is one reason why the world's believers are neatly referred to in the Bible as "children of promise"!

*   *   *

1

Lots of Them!

"I was flicking my way through my Bible when suddenly this verse leapt out at me. It seemed to be intended especially for me, and I felt that, somehow, the rest of my life wasn't going to be quite the same."

Words like this have been spoken countless times, as someone's natural resistance, or their comfortable agnosticism, has been shattered by one of God's promises becoming, all at once, intensely personal.

* * *

Whispers . . .

I was interested to find that there are at least a hundred and forty promises by God in the Bible. Those who have patiently researched this subject, however, have come up with even more. . . .

. . . In the New Testament alone, the researchers have found more than seven hundred verses in which a promise is implied, or reassurance given, or God's sheer dependability stressed.

God's promises have come to people in many different

ways . . . there wasn't always the Bible available! Although the ways of God's communication have varied, the result has usually been the same . . . a determination to believe the best of God, in a world which sometimes looks as if He has abandoned it.

So many of the world's great "achievers" seem to have plodded on in absolutely hopeless circumstances, with little more than a belief that God couldn't possibly let them down.

Amazing how those people, at least three thousand years ago, became aware of God choosing them, and making promises to them. . . .

God's very first intimations about Himself seem to have been in the form of an uncanny "awareness" (just as so many people find in the 1980s). . . .

Various individuals became conscious of being chosen to receive a kind of love-promise from God, as they felt His presence in solitary places, or in crisis situations. They seem to have received heart-whispers, rather than hearing a voice of thunder!

So often these were people in danger of starving to death; some had passions which kept landing them in all sorts of problems; some were totally misunderstood by families and friends.

These people became aware of God, somehow, whispering in their hearts what may have seemed, at the time, a rather extravagant promise.

The road towards the promises was frequently a lonely and discouraging one. In many cases, of course, the recipients (perhaps near to death), had to hand on God's promise, hand on their faith, having seen hardly any results! In spite of not fully experiencing what was promised, these people's lives had somehow been *fuelled* by

God's promises. And what a lot these characters achieved on the journey. . . .

In the sophisticated late twentieth century, people still find God whispering a promise, a sense of His dependability, in an intensely personal way. . . . Whether in the Arabian desert, or in a London bed-sit, it's the same experience.

* * *

Relevant

Just to keep a sense of realism, we'll need to look at some of the things which God has *not* promised us. . . . Also, we'll need to look at Divine promises with conditions attached (there are quite a few!)

These conditions, by the way, are not a sort of sinister bargain . . . promises with a catch to them.

God's "conditional" promises are rather like Mum saying, "Now, Mark, if you'll take care in the traffic, and remember your Green Cross Code, I'll have your favourite beefburgers and chips ready when you get in".

The "conditions" are based on exactly the same love which prompts God's desire to bless someone.

It's staggering to notice that although the many authors of the books in the Bible had no contact with each other, no knowledge of what the others had written, there's a definite "feel" to God's promises . . . as if from the same unmistakable source.

The contents of the promises have varied tremendously, of course. . . . There are promises of personal survival when violent death looked highly probable; promises about the recipient being greatly used in extending God's influence in the world. . . .

We can find promises about the basic necessities of life; about answered prayers; about strength beyond our own; about God living inside us; about freedom from personal "hang-ups"; about peace of mind; about seeing complex issues clearly; about an end to suffering.

Lots of Bible promises, as we know, are about the eventual arrival of the Divine Rescuer. . . . When Jesus our Lord came He was able to say "*Now*, you can see it all happening!"

You could somehow see God's continuing promise in the eyes of Jesus. . . . who then gave us quite a few more promises to hold on to (at which we'll be looking).

People receiving God's promises have ranged from the very simplest to the most sophisticated and articulate. God hasn't argued about His own existence, but wonderfully confided His plans to provide for us, and to find a way through life for us.

Many of the Bible words are addressed to specific categories of people . . . e.g. the afflicted, the searchers, the bereaved, the severely tempted. . . . We'll take a look at some of them, because their categories are still so relevant today, aren't they?

*   *   *

2

When They Light Up

God's promises haven't always been too precise about the details!! People have had to go forward, being certain of nothing except of God being able to cope. Those people gradually saw the inevitable obstacles and discouragements as irrelevant to what God would eventually achieve.

In His promises, God has given an unmistakable sense of His being the complete answer to the most complex human needs. What links *all* those promises in the Bible together is the basic thought of God's love not failing us.

In many of God's promises there's a definite challenge element. . . . "Are you *really* going to trust Me?" There has usually been this all-or-nothing aspect to the relationship with God, in moving towards realization of a promise.

*   *   *

Expecting. . . .

We find a wonderful thing happening when we take some of God's promises seriously. We find that trust in the promises gradually merges into a more-than-ordinary trust in the *Person* of God. For example, someone conscious of sharing life with Jesus may say, "I can't point to one specific promise on which I base my life. . . . I just know that He can't let me down!"

Once we've taken God's promises seriously, it doesn't matter if there's no specific promise, more than others, which has lit up for us, and which motivates us. . . . There'll always be a continuing promise *implied* . . . in the increasingly exciting relationship with a Person. Reliance on the promise has merged into reliance on all that God *is*. The warm acceptance of God's promises has proved to be the best possible starting point for really knowing Him.

It's interesting to look at those places in history where there's been intense spiritual brightness, with barriers to belief just crashing down. . . .

In such places, as God has begun to live in people's hearts, we'll find, somewhere, a promise-conscious person who has given God first place, and is expecting only the very best from Him.

In that rugged Old Testament character, or in that frail-looking but joyful young lady in the Ugandan missionary school, we see the same sort of thing. . . . We see mountains being moved – not by intense human effort, but by a power coming from "somewhere else": God's power operating in response to someone's willingness to trust, to receive from Him, and to allow Him to do one or two "impossible" things. The person concerned (probably quite "unimpressive") has done what God wants all of us to do . . . allowed no compromises and listened to no other voice, but just let a promise become a fact of life.

Jesus came to point the way for us, and gave us the opportunity to find a really extravagant trust in Him. He then proceeded to achieve so much through ordinary people who believed that He couldn't possibly fail them.

Great natural gifts haven't counted nearly as much as just relying on God and being available for Him to use.

Wonderful faith has centred around an *expectancy* about God. The expectancy hasn't been about desperately wished-for personal things, but about God bringing to pass what His purposes of love see as best in our lives.

* * *

Love-Sense

Every day, God is making a promise light up for the transforming of a person's existence. The faith to get hold of that promise is given simultaneously with becoming aware of it. The promise is built into the framework of a life, and affects it in all sorts of ways.

There's another remarkable thing about those who feel the "personal" nature of God's promises. Such people not only find themselves thanking God frequently for the eventual realization of the promise, but are able to detect ways, *now*, in which God is working it all out. . . .

It's sad that, for many "believers", a sense of God's remoteness may be due partially to a failure to reach out for one of those wonderful promises. There may be a failure simply to let one's life be a place where God works out His love-plans. There may be a failure to let

17

one's life be the scene of a trust relationship (perhaps laughed at a little by some) . . . a relationship in which God's sheer *dependability* is demonstrated, over and over again.

God's love is never more strongly felt than on a trusting journey started in response to a Divine promise. In fact, that consciousness of God's love is often felt as *in itself* part of the way in which the promise is being kept.

Just as we wouldn't (if we could help it) fail that child who slips a trusting hand into ours, so with God. Our recognition of His bringing us safely to this point in our life, and our belief in His *promise* to be with us until the world ceases to exist . . . these are foundations for our stepping out into the future.

God's promises (though seeming almost too good to be realizable when things are at their worst), are to be trusted . . . because they're built upon His sheer greatness. God is active all the time to work out those promises. We mustn't worry about those periods in which we can't notice His work. . . . We have to remember that there's His timing to be considered!

And, overshadowing all the other promises, is the hope that, if we trust God we will, at some future date, be with Him in a far brighter place. That's our goal.

Even in a book like this, quoting some of God's promises (which we'll do at the end of one or two of the chapters), can be a risky business. . . .

. . . .There's always the possibility that a promise (perhaps one with which we've been familiar for years) will suddenly light up for us. . . . It's then quite likely that we'll throw down the book (if we haven't done so earlier, in exasperation), and make plans to march off boldly in some new direction. . . .

18

When They Light Up

* * *

It's a wonderful thing if, in spite of all that's faith-destructive around us, we decide not to let go our trust in what God has got lined up for His children. . . .

His decision to bring about what is ultimately best for us has already been made!

* * *

3

Away He Went. . . !

Our chapter heading is borrowed from a modern Bible translation describing how someone in the Middle East, about 3,800 years ago, received a very personal promise from the mysterious God. Here's the verse:

> Abraham trusted God, and when God told him to leave home, away he went, not even knowing where he was going.

Well! The first question obviously is "Was Abraham a real person . . . or just an idealized personification of some tribal movements in that region?" You can sense some of the radical thinkers getting uneasy already.

Our answer to this question may depend on whether we accept the amazing fact of God existing at all in a universe like this. If we believe in God's existence, then perhaps it won't be too difficult to accept Abraham as a real person to whom God, so to speak, got through.

Events during that far-off period, such as Egypt's flourishing civilization, and the Jewish people's various comings and goings, are verifiable history, of course.

For God to "introduce Himself" to certain people in that period is a natural consequence of the fact that He exists . . . and that He's *interested*, don't you think?

The thought of God standing back from the people He has created, and never putting His arm around someone to communicate His love, sounds a little illogical. This impassive, unknowable God (whom many people, today, think we have to put up with) seems dangerously close to atheism at times.

It's much easier to believe that, in His love for His often failing children on this planet, God *has* reached out to them, from the earliest recorded times.

* * *

Breakthrough

It's interesting to notice the nature of God's first recorded communications with people on this planet.

These communications were not, as some have supposed, of the overwhelming "Big Brother is watching you" type, warning us not to step out of line. Although God did give rules for living, it would be easy to miss this wonderful promise-element when He made Himself known to people.

Those earliest contacts were promise-contacts . . . people were given, most decidedly, something to look forward to. It's worth looking at what happened to those Jewish wanderers, such as Abraham, his son Isaac, Jacob, Moses, Joshua, spanning the period from about 1800 to 1150 B.C. People who were far from perfect found that their own personal "supernatural breakthrough" was in the form of promises and encouragement!

God has repeatedly got through to individuals that they are not alone. He has made people very aware that they were in some way chosen to help out His plans. Those individuals have found a direction for their lives, as God has whispered to them about a way which they could follow.

How did He whisper? Good question!

Quite a lot has been written about God's promises and instructions to those Bible characters, but we may have been left wondering how on earth these things were communicated.

Was there a voice of thunder?

Was it those solemn, deep tones of the actor playing God in the more spectacular movies?

I don't think that we can rule out that there *was* a heavenly voice, an unmistakable voice. On the other hand, I am sure that God's making Himself known has been, essentially, a quiet intimation to the human heart. For example, it's possible that so many of the Jewish prophets received what they had to pass on from God in this quiet meditative way.

Mind you, there must have been some spectacular external happenings as well! God had to give some very tangible and clear signs to show people that there *was* Someone who could look after their interests in a dangerous world.

* * *

Away He Went. . . !

Going Somewhere

When someone makes a confident prediction about you, it gives you quite a boost, doesn't it? In the same way, God's predictions, His promises, gave those people in the Old Testament period something to keep them going in the often appalling conditions which they faced.

The sense of promise wasn't a sort of phoney encouragement, so that people would join up on God's side, but God's very necessary reminder, along a dangerous and uncertain road, of what He knew perfectly well He could carry out. That's why we're going to give a selection of God's promises at the end of chapters so that we can, if we wish, choose one or two, and start living by them straightaway.

Yes, it was a tough world for the earliest recipients of God's promises, but moving along the road God had shown to them, it wasn't long before they were able to share with families and friends a growing knowledge of the mysterious God.

Those early ambassadors for God quickly learned that they had to rely on Him completely. They realized how weak they were, and what tragic mistakes they made when they tried to do without God. Same today!

In those very challenging situations (moving into new and dangerous territory almost every few days), God's promise-people began to achieve some remarkable things. Others were soon to be amazed by how God's presence was affecting the lives of shepherds, and small nomadic farmers.

The way in which God got hold of people who may not have considered themselves particularly "spiritual", left them very sure about His existence, and that He had plans for them – and their families. These now became forward-looking people, once God had communicated his promises to them. They hardly knew where the next meal was coming from, hardly knew where they would end up tomorrow, but they knew that they were being taken *somewhere*.

Although the promise-recipients couldn't see what lay ahead, it was obvious that God had very good reasons for keeping this knowledge from them. One of the reasons, of course, was the development of their sheer trust.

The Hebrew wanderers were often under severe pressure to make diversions (they did sometimes!), but God usually brought them back to the route He had planned. The chosen leaders seemed to find an uncanny sense of being "steered by" this God whom they couldn't see.

*   *   *

One Eye On Us

As we know, God's promises were originally communicated within a particular sector of the world's population. It was in this sector that there began to emerge true knowledge of the God who had always been something of a mystery, and who has always been the subject of humanity's biggest question-mark.

But God's purposes, all along, were much wider – not to be restricted, in any way, to a spot at the eastern end of the Mediterranean! God has one eye on us, now, as we try to make sense of existence in the late Twentieth Century. He wants *us*, as well as Abraham and Co., to know that He is in the process of preparing a long-term future for us.

And so, the many promises in the Bible were put there for you and me, to make them ours. . . . If we make them ours we'll soon prove to ourselves that they are not just thoughts dressed up as God's by that priestly writer!

* * *

Promise-Content

What did God actually promise?

Well, basically, His promise was an amazing one . . . that people like us, with all sorts of failings, could enter into a relationship with the Spirit behind the universe. The sort of things which God "whispered" were:

"I'll be your God and you will be My people"

"I'll be a Father to you. . . ."

". . . You'll be My sons and daughters. . . ."

"I'll defeat those who try to oppose you. . . ."

"You'll have a long life and a great influence. . . ."

"I will live in you. . . ."

"I'll make you a holy people. . . ."

* * *

In addition to all this, as we know, God promised this refugee group a land reserved for His own identifiable people. On the way to possessing that land God promised miraculous help . . . including protection when the odds against the Hebrew wanderers seemed more than a little unfair!

* * *

Empty?

When we look at those rather extravagant sounding promises, and then at the hard facts of human existence, do those promises sound a little empty, a little unreal?

For example, what about God's promise to an insignificant group of Hebrews that all the nations of the world would be blessed through them? Incredible!

It must have seemed incredible at the time, but when shortly we look at how dependable the promises actually are, we'll realize that that promise is slowly but surely working out. It's not nearly as far-fetched as it must have seemed 3,800 years ago.

* * *

How did Jesus, who came on the scene 1800 years later, fit into all this? It's as if all those wonderful promises were set free to find their way into the minds of people everywhere . . . into yours and mine. Jesus came, not just to make the headlines, but to let people see for themselves God's sheer *reliability*.

Jesus was thinking hard about *us* when He said that

none of God's promises had become obsolete. This was because God's nature doesn't change. Those promises are just as fresh, just as relevant, towards the close of the twentieth century as when they were given.

* * *

And so, here's a very early promise . . . still speaking to you and me, if we'll let it. If we want to picture ourselves in Isaac's shoes for a few moments, I'm sure he wouldn't mind!

It's a good idea to allow a little time for this (and other promises quoted later), to sink in . . . and time to say a quiet, very personal "thank You" for them.

* * *

A PROMISE FOR TODAY

God says: "Don't be afraid. . . .
for I am with you. . . .
And I will bless you! . . ."

GRASPING THE PROMISE

Dear Lord, without knowing the details of the weeks and months ahead, I want to base my life on the fact of *You* . . . that You are with me.

I'm not sure how Your blessing will show itself, but I know that only good can come from Your companionship for the rest of my life.

Thank You for Your promise. In these few quiet moments, I make it mine.

DAILY REMINDER NO. 1

A "thank you" each day, based on the promises, acts as a useful reminder to ourselves, and guards against those inevitable mood fluctuations! . . .

Thank You, Lord, that I have nothing to fear because You are with me.

4

Why Me?

If we took a group photo of some of the people who have lived by God's promises, they would certainly look a very mixed bunch. . . . And yet, below the surface, God had seen that each one had certain very similar characteristics . . . and similar potential.

It's always a risk today, by the way, that God is looking very hard at one of us, and weighing up our potential!

* * *

Restless

God doesn't only give to carefully-selected people of "spiritual" temperament a sense of what He has in store for us (thank goodness!) Any of us, as long as our minds are not closed, can be swept off our feet, have our lives turned around, by God's promises.

It's exciting to reflect on the sort of people to whom the promises came . . . many of them virtual replicas of ourselves.

As we look at people who eventually made a tremendous impact on their surroundings, we can usually

29

find that the starting point was really a complete lack of complacency. They were *restless* people . . . people who knew that they needed something.

Some of those to receive a sense of promise from God were rebels . . . not exactly pious, gentle and obedient (we've only to think of how King David, Paul, Augustine and others used to be!) But God saw through all this, and observed the growing recognition of these people that they were incomplete. The "something" which they lacked (perhaps not fully realized by them), was God Himself.

In a way which we may not completely understand, God actually saw these people turning towards Himself before they themselves were conscious ever of feeling a need to do so. He saw their latent capacity to trust Him, uncompromisingly. This trust had to be of the nitty-gritty variety, not the pious, "comfortable" variety.

Starting perhaps with just one unforgettable experience, a love-whisper, that strong trust was developed (as it so often is, after a decisive "glimpse" of God). It was the sort of trust which remains even when, for the life of us, we can't understand what God is up to.

* * *

The Shy Ones, Too

And so, God had gradually to break the did-it-my-way element in His chosen ambassadors. These people, chosen to do great things, needed to allow God's very real control in their lives.

God's aim was that there should be a U-turn. He saw

these people become controlled achievers rather than self-willed angry young men. And they soon realized that it wasn't because of some special merit that they had been chosen.

Of course, it hasn't been just the fiery ones and the rebels! God's promises have also come to many shy uncertain people, feeling themselves very limited, and certainly variable in their faith (most of us?) But once again God sees beyond all this. God sees that in that rather apologetic and variable person there is one capacity, at least. That capacity is to be single-minded about the thing which matters . . . the desire for God.

So, looking at the recipients of God's promises on our photo, we could never detect the "logic" of choosing this particular lot. But God had been aware, already, of their arrival at a place He was preparing for them.

Later, a sense of God's presence made all the difference in the world to those promise-receivers. And, with the promise well and truly "buried" inside them, they were able to plod on (though hesitatingly at times!) along the road which God had made very clear to them.

In His unique way, God was also able to arrange that this sense of "destiny" did not violate their freedom of choice in everyday matters.

* * *

Compensations

We find that those who have a sense of living by a promise of God have times when they seem to have very little else *but* the promise! At one time they were fiercely tempted to envy people of prestige, affluence, power. But now that God has become mixed up in their lives, now that they're following a promise, they've stopped worrying about the things after which so many people strive. They have found a *better* ambition, even though they may have very little "going for them" in the worldly sense.

Don't you feel that there's a lot of what might be called "justice" about the way God intends to bless certain people? For example He has marvellously compensated, with a special sense of His loving presence, in cases of great suffering and handicap.

He has given inexplicable peace, and a sense of hope, to so many shattered by bereavement (often those who had no faith previously); He has promised love and understanding to those who have shown these things towards their friends . . . ("Blessed are the merciful"); He has promised to those who strive for sincerity, who are true to themselves, and to others, a lasting vision of Himself . . . ("Blessed are the pure in heart. . . ."); those who are misunderstood, or who are the victims of character assassination, are assured of a great reward in heaven.

It's as though, being aware of people's inevitable suffering in a hazardous world, but loving them so much, God has made up His mind to *more* than compensate . . . He promises (if we can hold on to Him) a complete end to human heartbreak. There'll be an unlimited experience of the very opposite of that heartbreak. Rather like a little child who has come through a tough time in hospital recently, finding that a super holiday has been booked by Mum and Dad.

Why Me?

Inevitable

To ensure just rewards for His children, it seems as if God has built into His universe a law in which things like compassion (even in some who may never see themselves as "religious") naturally attract to those who show them, the eventual realization of His promises.

And each trusting prayer, each deliberate choosing of God's way when an alternative would be more convenient, are inevitably attracting such promised rewards. Even if they're partially held up by the limitations and what seem to be the chance events of life, the promises themselves are unaffected. If we can trust God's dependability, we're going to enjoy, *for ever*, what He has carefully planned for us.

What happens when we take a firm grip on one of God's promises is that we find that we've "joined". . . . We've not necessarily become "Catholics" or "Protestants" or "Pentecostals". . . . We've joined a very distinguished group on which God sees no labels at all. We've joined the group which includes people like Abraham, Moses, Peter, Paul, Francis, John Wesley, Mother Teresa . . . people who have just moved, trustingly, with God, conscious that He can't fail them.

* * *

PROMISES FOR TODAY

"I'm going to give you a *new* heart . . . a heart of love."

"Your heavenly Father will always give you what you need from day to day, if you make the Kingdom of God your primary concern."

GRASPING THE PROMISES

Lord, I realize that I wouldn't be reading this if you hadn't seen me, already, as someone who can live by Your promises.

Thank you for the tremendous encouragement that failing people, just like me, have so often been given those promises.

I gratefully accept Your choosing of me. I gratefully accept Your promise, here, about meeting my needs, and about a quality of life which is completely different. I make those promises mine now.

DAILY REMINDER NO. 2

Dear Lord, thank You for choosing me. Thank You that right now You are making me into a new person.

5

Safety First

"I beg your pardon . . . I never promised you a rose-garden."

One of the hits of the 70s quoted a certain young lady's words to her disillusioned marriage partner. She added: "There's got to be a little rain sometime." Poor man!

Anyway, there are a number of things about which God can honestly say "I didn't promise you *that*, you know."

* * *

Every promise which God makes has a very specific purpose. That promise relates to the individual concerned and, beyond that, to many others whose future is also to be affected by His plans.

It's important, therefore, to notice the things which God has not promised . . . under any circumstances. For example, He has not promised that intense effort, inspired by human "wisdom" (with Himself left out), will automatically carry a result or reward.

Again, God has not promised short-term rewards in return for being on His side. The recipients of the promises have often experienced a long and testing wait. . . . Promise realization *can* be quick, but He doesn't promise that it will be.

God hasn't promised that we can completely ignore His loving commands and warnings and just dip into His lovely big box of promises! Even on the more mundane human level we'll usually try to be co-operative towards, or do little kindnesses for, someone who has left us a large sum in their will. . . . In God's case, however, the co-operation isn't just to butter Him up, in case He changes His mind. . . . It's to ensure our *safety*.

* * *

Walking Carefully

God's promises are to arouse a sense of what He has to offer compared with even the most seductive rewards of this earth. The long-term nature of most of the promises give us time to demonstrate just how trusting and loyal we can be.

The promises don't usually separate the great blessings God has lined up for us from the imperative to keep close to Him, to live gratefully, and to live with a sense of depending on Him for everything.

God has, in fact, given us a wonderful opportunity of using our free will to actually hurry along the realization of some of the promises! We can do this by our single-mindedness along the promise-road. There's more about this later, but for the moment can we notice that each kind act, each victory over our more negative moods, each time of waiting on God, all help along the realization-process? By contrast, our half-heartedness, or our compromising, can (without actually cancelling the promises) hold up their realization.

The things which God urged in His promises – the things He requires of us – all have to do with His amazing protection. Dangers have to be spelled out, warnings given, about those things which may seem attractive at first, but which eventually lead to separation from Himself.

* * *

If we look at the Bible "warnings" attached to some of the promises, we'll often find one about avoiding bad company and dangerous influences. We're warned against deliberately (even though realizing the danger) living for kicks. The tremendous drug problem is one of today's obvious examples.

From earliest times, God has got through to people how vital it is not to get mixed up in certain things and with certain types of person . . . "Separate yourselves from such people, and such influences", is a key theme.

There will always be temptations, of course, but we must not invite trouble by a compromising life-style (a common temptation of Christians). Certainly, God's promises are also held up when self-will gets the priority over quiet trust . . . another tendency common among Christian people, I'm afraid.

In his love God says, "Here's a plan for your life. It won't be easy. There'll be safety-rules. But you *can* see the plan work out if you'll remember those safety-rules."

The road which God has plotted is a very sure and

safe one, and *inevitably* leads to our receiving everything which He has promised.

You will have noticed how God lovingly makes us aware, usually by a loss of peace, that we're wandering into danger, or that we're clinging to something which conflicts with the promise-relationship.

We don't always realize that along God's promise-road there's always a present as well as a future promise-experience. There's an experience *now* of the peace, the love-sense, ultimately waiting for someone who has said, "Yes, Lord, I'll travel Your road". And we find that each time we want to keep to His road rather than wandering, it automatically brings what is required to make the choice involved.

The sense of God's control means that we've nothing at all to fear. We can trust His handling of situations and be ready for anything which life may throw at us. The way forward is His way, and the best way. Because God is over all created things, He's able to bring our needs and His own plans together in a beautiful way.

* * *

The Whole Package

Along the promise-road, there are constant little re-minders of the great blessings God has in store for us. We get these reminders each time we turn to God in our desperate need and find peace starting to come, each time we gently tell Him of our trust-in-spite-of. These things can happen in the darkest places – places when we may be tempted to think the promises too good to be realizable.

Every Christian knows that feeling of "illogical" peace projecting itself from one of God's promises into a present situation of suffering or confusion. It's a peace which says to us that in company with the promise-maker everything *must* turn out right. This is what happens when a true promise-sense has been developed.

We can be absolutely sure that the road, though hard, is one along which God will *only* permit what is right towards our eventual "promise-arrival". And along that road He'll save us from so much!

So don't let's ever see the conditions of the promises as God making the road one of unrelieved gloom and effort. On the contrary, we gradually find, to our surprise, that keeping on the promise-road is well within our capacity, and that this brings its own blessings, long before an actual promise is reached. Yes, there's an enjoyable as well as an effort side, once we've shown our consent to be "promise-children".

God's promises for us in the late twentieth century are not simply about pie-in-the-sky or jam tomorrow. We can cheerfully accept the whole package – promises and safety-rules – and go on to enjoy the walk with Him.

* * *

We find that God's commands, and His promises, both spring from His love . . . and blend beautifully. Like this:

"Be sure that you acquire wisdom."

"I'll guide you continually."

"Forgive your neighbour."

"I will lighten your darkness."

"Be of good cheer . . ."

"You will walk in safety."

"Do not be frightened."

"I will heal you . . ."

(I'm sure you can sort out the commands from the promises!)

An attitude of being happily resigned to God's promise-conditions is our solid foundation for all spiritual gains. It's the foundation for a wonderful sense of closeness which will follow. When we willingly accept those loving conditions – His safety measures – there's a uniting of His will with our own, and anything then becomes possible.

*　*　*

PROMISES FOR TODAY

GOD SAYS:

"HERE'S *your* part: tell the truth; be fair; live at peace with everyone; don't plot harm to others; don't say something is true when it isn't."

"Wear My yoke, for it fits perfectly, and you *will* find true rest of spirit."

GRASPING THE PROMISES

Dear Lord, I accept Your word that living by Your promises won't be easy. I realize, too, that living any other way will be even harder! Knowing me, You have worked out exactly the correct plan for my life.

Lord, thank You for the promise, here, about the peace which is mine as I keep within that plan. . . .

I make that promise mine now.

DAILY REMINDER NO. 3

Lord, thank You that through today You are working out in my life what is pleasing to You, and what is best for my future.

6

Non-Bouncing Cheques

"Rely on us . . . and relax!"

You can see this slogan on a fleet of those giant overnight parcels vans. It's a slogan which could have a lot to say to people who claim that they trust God and His promises.

*   *   *

"Rely on us . . . and relax! . . ." Unfortunately we don't always do either of those things. Among believers there can be a sneaky feeling that God's promises may not be in the category of hard facts. It seems safer to stick to the realities of existence. Far from relaxing, therefore, we feel that we must feverishly work out our own future.

"Too good to be true" may be our verdict as we look at those promises which God made, and then contrast them with the baffling world from which God seems, often, to be an absentee. Yes, God's words may seem hard to reconcile, at times, with life today . . . they may sound like a cosy ideal, more like a reflection of our own wishful thinking. And so we're tempted to say, "Looking at the place I've reached in my life, and the way things look like working out, God's promises seem an unlikely conclusion, to say the least."

The apparent contrast between promise and realism is, of course, the reason why those who have lived by God's promises have so often been treated with incredulity, or with a mixture of pity and contempt.

Even Christians of long standing may look at some of the Bible promises and wonder if they're fine-sounding words meant for someone else. And yet, if we say that we believe in God's love, and His greatness, it's logical to see the promises as just right for building our life upon.

Sadly, it has always been a minority who have *really* relaxed in God's sheer reliability.

* * *

Love Based

It's easy to make an empty or half-meant promise to change someone's will or intention, isn't it? And it's not only politicians who do it!

We're all inclined, at times, to promise things out of expediency . . . perhaps eighty or ninety per cent sure of carrying them out, but never being completely sure that we can. Even with the sincerest intention, human promises are, by their nature, limited, and exposed to failure. God makes promises, on the other hand, knowing exactly what He is up to in making them.

What we can often fail to see is that God, in performing miracles on our behalf, in His marvellous transforming of circumstances, does so not just because of His power. Those promises are *obligations upon*

Himself . . . obligations arising from His intense love for those He has created. This is the love which just can't help responding when one of us reaches out towards Him, perhaps in desperation.

It all comes down to something like a simple equation:

Love + Power = 100 per cent Dependability.

We can, therefore, bank upon the unlimited nature of God's promises . . . as unlimited as is His love. Because of that love we can be sure that God is at work, all the time, answering our urgent prayers in the best possible way. It's in times of great uncertainty that we can in fact be especially sure that He is at work on those promises! We find that those "illogical" predictions by God have a habit of looking increasingly realistic.

* * *

Solid

It was the American writer, Professor Glenn Clark, who described God's promises as being like blank cheques . . . cheques which did not bounce. "Never were gilt-edged securities issued by any corporation more certain than those promises. No fluctuations have ever been able to deflate their value", he said.

Professor Clark also very rightly pointed out that one of the great assets of God's "cheques" is that we can use them over and over again, with a different set of requests, as new circumstances arise.

God makes promises knowing that He is able to bring

all the complex facets of our life into an area of order and completion for us, if we'll accept those promises.

And so, God's promises are *not* empty; they are *not* illogical; and He's *not* capricious! Incidentally, God loves us to tell Him from time to time of our belief in His dependability. "Lord, I know You won't let me down", which has been said countless times through the centuries, is good for God to hear every day . . . and wonderful, too, for the deepening of our trust.

Those Hebrew wanderers blundered so frequently, didn't they? But that section of God's promises which was independent of conditions or of human attainment was not lost because of those blunders. As long as the road towards the promises was re-joined (rather like the motorway after a diversion), the promise stood.

Although those Old Testament characters let God down on many occasions, we can notice, so often, an agonizing depth to their sense of failure . . . which ensured God's response, as they looked to Him to lift them up again.

As we said earlier, it must have seemed an incredible promise to a rather scruffy, insignificant group of people, that through them the world's nations would be blessed. And yet that particular promise can be seen working out, can't it? The promise of God led directly to Jesus, and although there are still many who don't know Him, He has undoubtedly transformed, and is still transforming, the existence of millions in all races.

*   *   *

God has always stressed, and people have experienced, His integrity. He doesn't change His mind!

He doesn't change the promises when under pressure to do so . . .

He doesn't change the promises when it's more convenient for Him . . .

He doesn't change the promises when it's to His advantage . . .

He doesn't "tease" people with His promises . . .

When, with His knowledge of the future, God makes a pledge to us, that pledge stands. We can slow down the realization of those promises, as noted earlier, but the promises themselves are absolutely dependable. "God will never go back on His promises," wrote Paul, "He always does what He says."

I suppose, if it's not irreverent, we really could give God the title (among others) of "Mr Reliable".

* * *

Planning For Us

"I won't fail you." This message kept coming through to the leaders and the prophets of that chosen people. The promise of absolute dependability was more than just an encouragement . . . it had the motive of bringing someone to rely, completely, on Him. Soon there came the awareness of being cared for, and of being used. Even when what was happening around them seemed to spell out that God was a myth, there was that sense of their not being alone, and that the God who had broken through to them could be depended upon. "God shines for ever, without change or shadow" is how James later described it.

Just look at those "I won't fail you's" now, or perhaps at the words of Jesus our Lord about being with us always. There's a magic about them, if only we'll make them *personal* . . . they bring us closer. Those words help us to realize that God is going ahead of us, planning our meetings with people, making sure that nothing we encounter can do lasting harm to us.

Some of the world's evil influences threaten to stop us in our tracks, but God is the expert in actually making those influences increase our confidence in Him. What God has planned is completely unaffected by those influences and He doesn't let the development of our spiritual qualities be permanently checked by them. Soon our own lives start to show just a little of the sureness and the patience of God's working.

*　　*　　*

Mutual

Tucked away in God's promises not to let us down is optimism . . . that we won't let *Him* down! In other words, God is very ready to see dependability in one of us who is only conscious, perhaps, of fluctuating intention or of sheer inadequacy.

It's nice to be trusted, isn't it? It's a responsibility, of course, but nice! And God doesn't keep this feeling to Himself. He gives us, so often, the sense that in spite of our weaknesses, and misgivings, we are trusted by Him.

One of the surest ways to remind ourselves of just how reliable God is, is to think of the uncanny protection we have enjoyed through our life so far. The safe negotiation of places which filled us with apprehension. . . . The safe negotiation, I'm sure, of places which would have scared us stiff had we known the danger lurking in them!

Without God's dependability (stepping in to save us from what would hold up our progress towards His promises), it's doubtful if many of us would still be around to reflect on all this.

Just rely on Him . . . and relax!

* * *

PROMISES FOR TODAY

"I will not abandon you, or fail to help you."
"I won't change My decision to bless you."

GRASPING THE PROMISES

Dear Lord, You didn't make any of Your promises lightly. Thank You for Your promise here about Your sheer reliability.

Because of the sort of God You are, I know that You will never fail me, as I simply link my existence with Yours.

I make Your dependability-promise my own now. Thank You.

DAILY REMINDER NO. 4

Thank You, Lord, that I am in Your care today, and that You will not let me down.

7

Claim Them!

One of the saddest things is a life not shared with God. There are, of course, ultra self-sufficient people who feel no need of someone to lean upon, and certainly no wish for that someone to interfere.

But most of us are not quite as independent as all that, are we? There are literally millions who struggle through life bitterly, feeling that they're alone, and often deciding to get out of their difficult life prematurely.

* * *

God offers so much to people, but, for a variety of reasons, much of what He offers is unclaimed, and unused. It's only right to admit that God's promises haven't always been presented attractively and urgently by those who claim to represent Him. So often, what has been offered to people has been an intellectual discipline, or a code to strive after, or some rather barren ways of "service" . . . with just one or two reminders of God on the way, if we're lucky.

Hundreds of thousands have been turned away from even the thought of God by such a presentation. "Allowing God in" can mean to some people allowing in also deprivation, stoicism and a general absence of joy! God's blessings, they feel, belong either to the distant past, or to the merely wishful future.

* * *

Change To Hope

It is vital to take God's promises very seriously as affecting our life *now*. If the promises are not taken seriously and claimed, if there's only a partial sharing of what God is, our "religion" can become more of a minus than a very definite plus.

The major promise from God (which doesn't always come across as the personal experience of those passing it on!) is that we can *know* that we're greatly loved. The promise is that we can feed upon what, for many of us, is the only source of love in our life.

Fortunately, in spite of wishy-washy presentation, God finds ways of giving a glimpse of something better to most people . . . unless their minds are closed by a fixed wish to run life their way, or by a supposed intellectual superiority.

If we say that God plays a part in our life, it must mean that there's now a life-changing hope which wasn't there previously. This change must be more real than if someone promised to give us a share of their fortune a few years from now!

The grand strategy of supernatural evil forces is to try, at all costs, to prevent God finding, and then keeping, a place in our hearts. I'm sure that some of the more oppressive atheistic regimes throughout the world have been "used" in this way. If the supernatural powers of evil can get human beings to laugh at the thought of a caring God, then they feel that they are succeeding.

But God has all sorts of ways of reaching people! As we know, there are countless secret and not-so-secret followers of Jesus in those "religionless" countries. One of the main reasons for Jesus keeping alive in the hearts of these brave people is that they base each day on His promises and His dependability. In an often grim existence, the promise-sense makes all the difference.

* * *

Just think of some of the things which God offers to us which can often go unclaimed – perhaps for almost a lifetime:

> The opportunity to let the circumstances of life be *expertly* shaped for our ultimate good.

> The opportunity to have that relaxed dependency on Someone infinitely able to cope.

> The peace of mind of knowing that our loved ones who have died are in that promised land of safety.

> The knowledge that because we've accepted a promise, God is blessing and using all that comes our way.

> The definite feeling that the dream we once had of becoming "a real Christian" is moving closer to realization!

The chance to share God's *companionship* on the promise-road, and to "take in" a little more of Him each day.

A sense of continuity . . . a very logical awareness of life with God *going on*. . . .

A sense that as we move towards a promise, God is not only meeting our day-to-day needs, but anticipating them. . . .

The gradual removal, as we bank upon His promises, of that paralysing guilt which can haunt even the most "confident" person. . . .

All that is promised . . . and lots more.

Yes, it's tragic that God's promises are so often seen by theologians and many "professionals" as rather outdated Bible oddities. It's tragic when a Christian life, lacking that promise-sense, fails to make others want to share that sort of life.

* * *

Motivation

Talking to seriously ill people, you realize just how many promises are claimed near the very end of life, when what the world can give in temporary support is recognized for its inadequacy. From God's point of view, of course, the great sorrow is that those lives have been lived without that sense of "going somewhere".

Every Christian can find it well worth checking, frequently, that God's promises have been *fully* claimed, and that they don't remain in the sphere of mere wistfulness.

Before reading on, could we make a quiet promise to ourselves . . . ? When we're confronted by a Divine promise, from now on (whether it's something we hear, or something we read), let's literally grab it, and make it our life's motivation. Don't let us fail through procrastination or half-heartedness. There's a promise almost challenging us to accept. We mustn't let it slip away.

Just think of it . . . we've put our arms around a promise! We're not listening any more to the voice of doubt (based on past failures and disappointments), but to the voice of God.

The presence of **Jesus** will now be more real than the fluctuating details of each day. We'll now see Him working out situations in a way which we failed to see before those promises became our property.

*   *   *

PROMISES FOR TODAY

Jesus says:

"My purpose is to give eternal life . . . abundantly."

"For those who are thirsty, there exist springs of life-giving water . . . as My gift."

GRASPING THE PROMISES

Dear Lord, help my way of life to be free from all distortions about the sort of God that You are.

Help me to base my life firmly upon Your promises, and especially the love which lies behind them.

Help me not to let any promise go unused.

I believe Your promise of a new kind of life and, knowing that it is for me, I claim that promise now. Thank You.

DAILY REMINDER NO. 5

Thank You, Lord, that my life today is *being affected* by the promises which I've claimed.

8

Told You So!

There's a little verse in the Bible about those who have God sharing their lives. Here it is, in a modern translation:

> "They don't need to own property . . . the Lord is their property!"

Yes, the real wealth for a person to possess is *God Himself*.

*   *   *

When Jesus "visited" our planet in that special way, the sense of possessing God was brought much closer for us. All God's love, all His beauty, were brilliantly lit up and made available. People saw something which those Old Testament characters would have given their right arms to see . . . the Maker of the Promises! Here He was, now completely involved in His creation.

Suddenly, those ancient promises were not so remote, not just fine words, not a little hard to believe any more. People could now *see* the Promise-Maker wonderfully at work in all that Jesus did. The God of those promises in the desert had, all along, been "doing business" with us through His Son!

Remember what Jesus said? . . . "Before Abraham was, I AM." Abraham and Co. had been experiencing *Jesus*. As S

Paul said later, "They were all sustained by the spiritual rock which followed them everywhere. That Rock was Christ!"

When Jesus came, the love which lay behind the promises of God could be seen plainly . . . seen in all the healing miracles, and seen, of course, on the Cross.

People (even the "religious" ones), who had long wondered whether there was another dimension to life apart from the material, could now see that there was. It was no longer a case of "We understand that God once told our ancestors that He loved us" but "We now *know* that He does".

If Jesus had said "I told you so" (many of His statements virtually amounted to this), He would have been absolutely on target. Yes, Jesus, in a wonderful way, *became* God's promises. As Paul wrote later, everything promised to those ancient Hebrews had now come through to us: "Jesus Christ carries out and fulfils all of God's promises – no matter how many there are", he said.

Wasn't it a dramatic change in the "feel" of God's promises when Jesus came? "Fear of" gradually became "friend of". A new dimension to the promises had come. The writer of the letter to Jewish Christians commented that Jesus's coming had, in fact, meant "far more wonderful promises" to be grasped.

Yes, not only were those original promises brought excitingly alive, but Jesus gave us some more to hold on to! These promises of Jesus were often directed towards us being *part of Him* . . . Jesus actually living in us. His dearest wish was, and still is, that we should arrive at a sense of being in some way united with Him . . . this gradually merging into a complete realization.

God's Promises

"If you 'belong' to Me, all that God is, and all that He has promised, are *yours*", is what Jesus was saying.

*   *   *

Love's "Sternness"

There's no doubt that the promise-message of Jesus was also a stern one! The road towards what God had prepared had to be very narrow, in view of the variety of seductive roads leading away from really knowing Him. And, sadly, some of these existed, and still exist, in organized religion.

People who had been tempted to see God's promises as possibly the dreams of an old scribe, and certainly not for them, could now say "Hey! It's all true, after all!"

*   *   *

There For Us

When Jesus's brief "visit" was over, He made sure that God's spirit was, so to speak, let loose in the world, convincing people of the love-base of those promises. Jesus's appearance was the climax of that journey patiently taken by those Old Testament promise-recipients. At the same time it was the start of another journey for people like us . . . who may never have been near Palestine in our lives!

Yes, Peter, John, Andrew, Matthew, the sick, the emotionally burdened, the down-and-outs, were seeing what their ancestors had longed to see . . . the fullest expression possible in earthly conditions of God's love and of His invincibility. If your heart hadn't been corrupted by worldly standards, or by pride, in the name of "religion", it was all there for you!

How fortunate were those who were expectant, like children, and who could welcome Jesus with open arms. How deprived were those of a detached and sceptical attitude – either then, or today.

When Jesus read out in the synagogue that passage from one of the promise-receivers (Isaiah), about release for the captives and sight for the blind, His comment was: "These scriptures came true today!"

If we notice a real danger towards which a child is heading fast, we don't continue sitting there and say limply, "Er, excuse me, my dear . . . I wonder whether you'd mind watching out for danger in the next few moments?"

The hopes which Jesus gave to us were set in an uncompromising and very urgent message. The message was stern, but was essentially protective . . . He could see dangers which we can't.

Shining through the message of Jesus our Lord, with its imperative call to walk in God's ways, is always a promise of love and security. These are now the promises of a Friend . . . the mysterious Godhead now includes, within itself, profound appreciation of our existence on this planet. God couldn't (even if He wished) look with detachment upon our conflicts. What happens to us is always very near to His heart.

*　　*　　*

Is it possible to test for ourselves the reliability of the promises which Jesus made? Well, here are just a few examples:

> A promise that the Church He began with a handful of working-class followers would go from strength to strength, and that anti-God forces would never be able to crush it. . . . Incredible, but it has come true!

> A promise, just before facing execution, that His friends would see Him again. . . . Incredible (dead people usually remain that way) . . . but on Easter morning it came true!

> A promise to His followers that they would receive power, and do the sort of things He had been doing. . . . Incredible (just ordinary fishermen), but around the Mediterranean, soon after the Resurrection, it came true!

* * *

God's Plan Working

We've already noted how so many of Jesus's remarks had that extra dimension. He knew that what He said in contemporary situations would be recorded by Spirit-inspired followers . . . those reporter-evangelists!

Jesus not only gave us that promise of being united with Him in the closest possible way. He also gave us the promise of something priceless . . . something which even today's most sceptical and "independent" people would love to think could be theirs. Jesus promised us something new . . . eternal life! He intended this to be a little foretaste of heaven in our present existence. After this foretaste, there's absorption into a *permanent* state of knowing Him and enjoying Him.

The coming of Jesus meant a strong light for us along the promise-road; it meant unique help in experiencing all that God has planned for us. That coming was the supreme moment at which human longings, questions, and even bitterness, met up with God's love.

All God's promises, carefully handed down through those Jewish families, now had that special quality . . . you could actually see them working out. Yes, Jesus offered Himself as the great turning-point for all of us. Whatever our personal make-up, we can tread the road which Jesus now lights up. We are also power-assisted, of course, by the same Person!

* * *

Already Ours

It's vital for promise-recipients to keep Jesus (as the personification of those promises) as the focus of our attention. We need look nowhere else for those very deep desires to be met . . . even though many things appear to be the answer. Jesus, as both the origin and the goal of those promises, is the natural place to which we can turn when any need arises. If we're really determined to share in God's promises it's always worth checking "Is Jesus first? Is He my chosen companion?"

Each single moment spent in the presence of Jesus our Lord, lovingly thinking of Him, is a very definite step along the promise-road. When we eventually achieve those promises, all present hurt, emptiness, futility-sense will vanish. Until that time we've got that "illogical" but wonderful sense of hope because Jesus is with us. None of the world's temporary solutions can provide a hope of that sort.

God has "tailored" His promises to meet those deep wishes of individuals (so deep in some people that they won't admit to having them!) *Only* Jesus can both promise and carry out so unerringly. Once Jesus shares life with us, we have all that we really need. Lying ahead of us is the time when what is already ours is able to be enjoyed without all the conflicts, and sense of incompleteness, of our present existence.

What a wonderful thought that for any person today, Jesus *is* God's promises. Promise-recipients find all their ambitions narrowing down to just one: possessing Jesus. His love gets to the centre of our life, and everything now starts from that place.

For most people it's hard to visualize some blissful future existence for very long, without the intervention of "realism" and pessimism. But possessing Jesus makes such a future look extremely likely after all!

* * *

PROMISES FOR TODAY

Jesus says:

"I am the Bread of Life. . . . No one coming to Me will ever be hungry again."

"I am the One Who raises the dead and gives them life again."

"If you believe in Me, even though you die like anyone else, you will live again. You are given eternal life. . . ."

GRASPING THE PROMISES

Dear Lord Jesus, as I look at You I begin to realize that You are not only the Maker of the promises, but that You *are* the promises.

I realize that if my life is completely given over to You, those promises are *automatically* mine.

Thank You for Your promise, here, to meet my spiritual needs on this earth, and then to lead me beyond this present existence.

Right now, I make that promise mine.

DAILY REMINDER NO. 6

Lord Jesus, thank You that today I have *all* that I really need by possessing you.

9

Rolled Into One

Possessing Jesus! Once we're aware that not only do we belong to Him, but that He belongs to us, a very exciting situation exists. When we said that having Jesus as our friend meant possessing all of God's promises, it wasn't just a play on words. Our trust in the Divine promises really does progress naturally, as we said at the beginning, to trust in a Divine person.

When we're lucky enough to have a very special human friend, we have much more than a friend, don't we? There's much more than a companion, or someone to talk to. We also have all that the friend *is*, all that our friend has to give in his or her nature, or talents.

So it is, on a much larger scale, of course, with Jesus. When He's "ours", we become more and more aware that we have all sorts of gifts which God has long awaited us to have.

* * *

Rolled Into One

Consolidation

When dear old headstrong Peter took those few steps on the surface of the lake towards Jesus, I'm sure that the promises and inspiring words from his Master weren't exactly on his mind. What was driving him forward in that mad moment of defying gravity was, of course, the Person! (By the way, I'm convinced that this incident really happened and is no exaggeration, in view of the amazing events of those three years, aren't you?)

Anyway, it's vital to realize that having Jesus as our property, so to speak, automatically ensures that the qualities we'll need in order to feel at home when we reach that place called heaven are becoming ours. To have made many of the promises ours . . . that's great. But we need those promises *consolidated* by our conscious possession of Jesus as life's companion.

In a sudden crisis, a prolonged anxiety situation, it could be that a promise of God by which we've eagerly lived will seem to fade a little. The words which once inspired us may not do so now. It's not that "our" promise has been lost, of course . . . but being flesh and blood, there might, under stress, be a temporary remoteness about it.

It is in those dark places, therefore, that our instinctive trust will usually switch to the *person* of Jesus. When the crisis passes, or we start coming to terms with a situation, there stands the promise . . . ready to motivate us again. When we lose for a time our sense of direction, when the promise-road seems to get itself lost in fog conditions, we so often find that God has laid on for us a compensation. . . . That compensation is a stronger sense of His person, a greater unity of His own heart with ours.

Peter once said to Jesus, "Where in the world *can* we go except to You?" It's this trust in Jesus's person which will hold us up, when perhaps some of the promises don't look like working out, and there is temporary darkness. There are going to be times when what is left of our reasoning capacity can grasp only one thing . . . the love of Jesus and His responsibility for us. We may hardly be able to live with our sense of failure, the future may seem too awful to contemplate, but we find ourselves able to cling to our one priceless possession . . . Jesus.

* * *

Still Shining

I have spoken to many people who have grown bitter after life's tragedies. Some have defiantly asserted that it's wrong to hope for anything, and that faith is an illusion. Certainly, hope can almost vanish, even for Christians, but I don't think that it is ever totally extinguished. It's an "unjustified" hope, of course, in many people's view. But for us who have put our life in the hands of Jesus, that one solid place is never more noticeable than when existing supports start to crumble.

When there's great fear, when we've lost someone greatly loved, when a dream has been shattered, there's usually just one source of light . . . Jesus, the promise-maker. Through the darkness enveloping our journey we see His light. That light assures us that we're still on the promise-road, and that one day (though perhaps not just yet), we'll be steadily moving along it again.

"Master," said Peter, "You've got the words of eternal life." Yes, but, deep down, Peter's trust had become fixed on Jesus, even more than upon His words. . . .

There's something all-inclusive about having Jesus . . . who is all the promises rolled up into one. It's in possessing Jesus that those spirit needs can be met without waiting for heaven! There is available to any personality a vital change ingredient in our current circumstances. His ability to meet needs is why He refers to Himself as the Bread of Life.

In the eyes of Jesus our Lord, there's no such thing as a "difficult" human temperament, or an "impossible" human situation. What He does with such temperaments and such situations only serves to show how wonderful He is.

* * *

It can be staggering to reflect, from time to time, "The Person I'm trying to follow, the Person whose promises I'm trusting, is the origin of everything which I see around me." No wonder we can rely on His promises! No wonder that there's the sense, in daunting circumstances, that if we possess Jesus the best is yet to come.

Having found the maker of the promises we begin to find, of course, that so elusive quality of peace. Finding the maker of the promises, we begin to discard some of those temporary "solutions" which are so plentiful today.

Jesus gives us a deep and instinctive knowledge, defying analysis, that God's promises *must* be moving towards realization.

* * *

PROMISES FOR TODAY

"Here on earth you will have many trials and sorrows, but take courage . . . I have overcome the world."

"If you follow Me, you won't be stumbling through the darkness. Living light will flood your path."

GRASPING THE PROMISES

Dear Lord, I believe that all mankind's hopes, its deep longings of the spirit, are never quite satisfied here, but start to be realized when we are really aware of having You.

Thank You that all the promises light up, if I possess You.

Thank You for Your promises, here, to guide me through life, and to help me to win victories.

I make them mine now.

DAILY REMINDER NO. 7

Lord Jesus, thank You that You know the way through today, and that nothing can defeat You.

10

Action Needed

By this stage, we have (I trust!) made one or two of the promises well and truly ours. Perhaps we can even quote some to our friends, if this happens to be the sort of thing we find easy! . . .

What, then, is the vital next step? Well, of course, that much needed next step is the active building of our own particular promises into everyday existence.

You'll know how something which Jesus said can produce a warm feeling, a hopeful feeling, which so often contrasts with current problems . . . This means that His words are transcending time, transcending their original context. Those words are contemporary and relevant every time we read them.

It's when we *act* on those words that they turn out to be precisely what we have been needing all through our life! These words have an uncanny way of being relevant to any situation we're in. Immersing ourselves in those words, we're in contact with God's present love, His present wisdom and His present power.

In no possible way are the truths contained in God's word out-dated, nor have His intentions for us changed one bit.

It makes a tremendous difference when we've made a promise ours, and (knowing that God's nature doesn't change), begin to let that promise drastically affect our present way of living. It's never too long before we find that acting on a promise *works*!

It's worth keeping in mind that in helping us to act on a promise, God pledges His *companionship*. Our promise-journey is with a companion Who has every combination of circumstances at His finger-tips. No real ethical attainment is possible without that companion (how often Christians choose to ignore "Without Me you can do nothing"!) It's exciting to realize that companionship is promised which stretches as far into the future as we can visualize . . . and this gets one or two earthly "harsh realities" into proportion a little.

As we warmly accept a promise and make it part of us, God simply wants us to keep close, and therefore safe. The journey to the promises is all about the indivisibility of ourselves and God . . . stretching towards that place of realization. If, like children, we have warmly accepted His promises, He'll never stop working in us to turn good intentions into action.

Yes, we may even begin to feel a quiet joy at the unknown (perhaps hazardous looking) future, because it's going to be shared with him.

* * *

Action Needed
Power-Influence

You know, it's more than just a promise which God gives us. We begin to realize that we're under an *influence* . . . and we can sense this influence, even when we're reading His stern bits! This love-influence is rather like a circle around our life, something in which we can just let ourselves go, allowing it to dominate. *His* ambition (even stronger than ours), when making the promises, is simply, our happiness . . . even though the road through earthly imperfections and fluctuations may be rough. Just like those Bible characters, we can now begin to move through life upon God's promise that every obstacle is going to be conquered for us. Even an imperfect, "growing" trust in the promise-maker ensures, automatically, His invincibility being at our disposal. And we won't in the least mind having Him in charge of things as each day we move a little closer to promise-realization.

And so, the great secret of living by God's promises is allowing what He communicated to His chosen instruments through the years to lift us *now* above our limiting circumstances. What lifts us is the *power* which lives within a promise – especially when that promise has been welcomed!

God longs to bring you and me into that group of people whose lives are completely changed by His loving *control*. No, we don't have to wait to "improve" a little before grasping any of the promises. And grasping doesn't lead us into a world of unreality and misplaced efforts. . . .

Grasping the promises helps us, as nothing else can, to begin that close walk with the Promise-Maker.

Hooked!

Hard to say, precisely, what has made so many people take a promise of God – printed in the Bible, repeated in a talk, quoted in a book – and make it their own. I'm sure that on such occasions God *gives* something unique and very necessary. Beyond logical argument, God gives to us, first of all, a sense of the sheer dependability of His promise . . . plus a sense of His own absolute dependability. It is this whisper of God, as we read or listen to a promise, which motivates us. The promise gets hold of us . . . we're hooked on it!

God sees something when the reliability of a promise lights up inside us . . . He sees us starting (at last) to make our life change from one of wanting to one of achieving.

Let's say that we've looked hard at a promise (for example, "I will lighten your darkness", from the Old Testament . . .) What do we make of it? Is God giving us a sense that it is especially for us? If this is the case, it's a good idea to *thank* Him straight away, even before we've thought out some of the implications of the promise!

Thanking God has clinched that promise for us. We now begin to see some of our problems, some of our failure areas, in the light of that promise.

Into the different situations, present and future, we'll now *expect* the Lord to bring some brightness. . . . The promise will remind us, at times of stress, that we've light to which we can turn. We'll not only remember the promise at such times but will *experience* from Him, Who is the source of light, that "hope-in-spite-of" feeling. We're *acting* on a promise, not just remembering it.

We often wonder why some Christians, living in the

most mundane circumstances, have such radiance and thankfulness. Well, in so many cases, they have a hidden source of their gratitude . . . they're now acting on God's promises to them, and finding that they work.

Often, we'll find it hard to believe that we, too, have become promise-recipients but, in fact, His decision to light up some promises for us was made a long time previously! He saw our need and saw, as well, something which we may not have seen . . . a capacity to follow Him, resolutely, along the promise-road.

Looking back, those now living by God's promises can see how He had been drawing their thoughts towards Himself over a long period, ready to reach out with a life-changing promise. The sense of gratitude about God's planning for us in this way can be overwhelming.

* * *

Promises Applied

So, we've made a few exciting-sounding promises ours!

It's vital that, straight away, our life should become a promise-reflecting one. Our choices, our braver reactions to circumstances, our relationships, our surprisingly bold advances in some specific challenging areas . . . these can now have God's promises as their foundation. We're ready to let trust stop becoming just a word. That trust can now be of the sort which actually recognizes Jesus keeping His promises in all "chance" incidents and "chance" meetings, in those "chance" occasions of people being helpful towards us.

It's a marvellous experience to be able to look at a day's

happenings and say to oneself "Hey! . . . *that* was God keeping His promise!"

As soon as possible, God's promises must be brought into the pattern of our life . . . even if only partially at first. The important thing is that *some* area is affected by a promise, soon after making it ours. For example, "In the world you will have trouble and sorrow, but cheer up . . . I have overcome the world." That promise can result in a little extra courage, a little extra patience, a little extra hope in a current situation.

Our embracing of God's promises plays a key part in God being *seen* at work in us, and in our circumstances. Yes, He'll be seen at work by those who are used to noticing these things, even if we ourselves feel very little spiritual prestige!

*   *   *

Challenge

By the way, it's always a temptation to "share" . . . perhaps a little self-indulgently. We need not be in a hurry to convince others, right from the start, that we're promise-motivated. There's a quiet but vital consolidation period in which our response to God's promises will be known only to ourselves. Opportunity to tell others all about it will come. . . . "The Lord told me this morning" can sometimes wait for a little while.

As we know, life so often comes down to a series of choices. In many of these choices, for the promise-follower, there's a challenge element: believe that God's victory is yours on *this* occasion . . . or be fatalistically resigned to the existing reaction pattern. We can now meet those challenging choices with our own special promise echoing inside us. The Maker of the promise and we, together, turn a victory-promise into a victory-demonstration. It's so sad when we temporarily abandon our confidence in a promise when victory is within our grasp. . . . God would not have let us down!

* * *

PROMISES FOR TODAY

God says:
"When you go through deep waters and great trouble I will be with you; when you go through rivers of difficulty, you will not drown!"

"Be sure of this . . . I am with you, always, even to the end of the world."

GRASPING THE PROMISES

Dear Lord, I can see that it's not enough to read Your promises with interest, or merely to analyse them. I believe that Your promises really do transcend time, and have a special purpose . . . that I should live by them now.

I believe that *all* Your promises relate in some way to my life. Please light up the promises on which my immediate future can be based.

Thank You for the promise, here, about Your companionship and Your protection. I make them mine now.

DAILY REMINDER NO. 8

Lord, thank You that whatever the obstacles today, You will lift me above them.

11

We Break Ours!

"Sorry, Lord, You must be sick of hearing me promise this. But here it is again."

During a lifetime, the number of promises in the reverse direction (*to* God) which we make and break must be frighteningly large. So many broken promises which need repeating . . . including, I'm afraid, some which we made rather lightly in the first place.

* * *

Thought Through

When we're really conscious of God's promises to us, there's an instinct to reciprocate. Although we go on to break so many of our promises, and fail in our good intentions, it's nevertheless a good instinct to make those promises (as we'll see in a moment).

What really matters when we fail, of course, is *His* promise to us. Although God is naturally hurt by those times when we let Him (and ourselves) down, He has arranged it that our journey can be continued. His own unwavering promises (though we feel so unworthy of them at failure-times,) give us that upsurge of confidence, that encouragement to begin again.

We will have far fewer failures if only we'll carefully think through the promises we make to God. There's a temptation to make a promise lightly, with the thought at the back of our mind that there's always an escape-route, a begin-again chance.

And so, before saying "Lord, I'm going to ____" or "Lord, You can certainly rely on me to ____", we ought to face, for a few moments, what it might cost in things like effort, or absolute trust, when choices conflict.

Before promising, it's worth remembering that it won't be exactly easy, in view of the tremendous pressure to put aside our good intentions. The very frequent failures which happen when promises have been lightly made can make us terribly vulnerable people. Realizing that we made a glaring exception to a promise which we could so easily have kept, in His strength, can temporarily affect that sense of moving upwards with our Companion. We had courage there, but didn't use it; we acted without God; we didn't consolidate; we just didn't *use* Him.

* * *

Promise-Memory

In view of what we've said, are promises made to God of very little use? On the contrary: even a promise which gets broken occasionally is important! It is, in fact, the *memory* of our promise which so often in "difficult" areas drastically reduces the number of failures. Having a promise of our own to live up to means that we'll at least try, if not always succeeding, and God will see progress.

The memory of a promise which we've made to God will often come flooding back to us when there's one of those crucial choices. This memory will help us, for example, to act lovingly and generously towards someone, when we don't feel in the least like doing so. The memory will help us in countless ways.

Yes, the instinct to make promises of our own is a good one (as long as we weigh them seriously) and *must* mean lots of gains among those flops!

There's one promise, above all else, which I think it's vital to make, one we can usually keep. This is it: "Lord, I'll never turn away from You, whatever happens, as the main hope of my life."

Failures will come, but that promise at least can be fixed, just as His, to us, are fixed.

* * *

We know what a harsh existence it was for those writers of the Psalms (assassination was often just around the corner!), but listen to some of their promises to God:

"I will worship You with deepest awe."

"I will always be glad because of You."

"I will always trust in You, and in Your mercy."

"O Lord, my God, I will keep on thanking You for ever."

"I will tell everyone how great and good You are."

"When I'm afraid I will put my confidence in You."

Our almost instinctive promises to God to make Him our hope, to put Him first, are what He looks for when starting to show us what a difference it can make if He shares our life.

When we fail in *specific* areas ("Lord, You know that I didn't resist that cigarette") we can be sure that He's not forgetting that *overall* promise of ours about Him having first place. This means that we can always bank upon that source of strength – if only we'll use it – to keep the more specific promises.

Seeing what you do see in hospitals, by the way, you soon realize what a sensible promise the no-smoking one is!

The very fact that we've made an "overall" promise about God coming first will always help us to build something out of the failure-moments in the specific areas.

How fortunate we are that God has "allowed for" our breaking many promises. As long, that is, as we remember that there's danger if, knowing this, we continue to make them too lightly.

The great thing is that although our promises may collapse, His love does not. It's that sense of God's love which helps our determination to be more firm about a promise which we may have broken a few times already.

* * *

We Break Ours!

Seeing Beyond Failure

Peter (we seem to quote him quite a lot!) blurted out, "Lord, at least you can count on *me*. . . . You know I'd die for you." Jesus replied, with His Divine insight, that Peter would, in fact, prove disloyal in a moment of challenge.

When this denial of Jesus eventually occurred, it could well have been that suicide crossed Peter's mind. But, of course, Peter's basic overall loyalty and intention were well-known to Jesus. In spite of that let-down, Jesus kept looking at Peter's basic intention and, after coming back from the dead, beautifully kept His promise to build His Church on Peter.

The Divine promise stood, even when a rather emotional and extravagant promise by Peter failed miserably. Jesus still looked at what was in Peter's heart. And so Peter could now live with himself again because Jesus had seen beyond that one failure. That was to encourage *us*, I'm sure!

There'll be many tricky places in the future when we'll be forced to say to ourselves, "It's sure not easy to follow Jesus here . . . but somehow I'm glad that I've *promised* to do so."

Let's not forget, when failure comes, God's continuing trust in us to go on moving towards those promises. All this will help us to return very quickly to Him when finding that we've begun travelling in a wrong direction.

The promise of heaven was not for perfection (thank goodness!), but for persistence.

* * *

A PROMISE FOR TODAY

"Be glad if you're hungry and thirsty to do what is right. You are going to be fully satisfied."

GRASPING THE PROMISE

Lord, I'm aware of so many broken promises. I'm sure that You must be tired of hearing some of them repeated.

Help me never to lose that *desire* for You in my heart, that desire to please You.

Thank You for Your promise, here, to encourage me in *persisting*. I make it my own.

DAILY REMINDER NO. 9

Thank You, Lord, that I have the strength which I need today to keep *all* my promises to You.

12

Built-In Help

Listen to that swaying mass of fans at the football game singing "You'll never walk alone". . . .

Sadly, there won't be too many who are thinking about God as they sing those words! The lyric of the song nevertheless sums up one of Jesus's most beautiful promises – that God's Holy Spirit would come and live in His followers.

Keeping God's promises firmly in our vision will need both strength and an awareness of Himself, and this is why Jesus said that the Holy Spirit would take the promise-road with us.

* * *

Involved

As the Spirit of God fills more and more of our life, the obstacles and the wrong turnings simply won't be able to get in the way of our progress. Jesus, living in us by His Spirit, begins to make our intentions His, and the route taken towards the promises then becomes the best possible one.

It's very important to keep in mind that *indivisibility* of the Promise-Maker and the Promise-Companion. God the Father, initiating creation through His Son (and later sharing human existence through Him), is experienced in two amazing ways. . . . Firstly, He fills the whole universe; secondly, He makes His home in the heart of anyone on this tiny planet who will dare to believe in Him.

It's very much as if the risen Jesus says to us, "I'm glad that you've set out on this promise-journey. If you don't mind, I'll sit beside you and see that you don't get out at the wrong station before the journey is completed."

In making some of God's promises ours, we have, so to speak, "qualified" for the state of unity with Jesus which He called eternal life. But we'll always need, desperately, the close involvement of the Promise-Maker. . . . I don't think that we always appreciate that one of the main reasons for Jesus visiting this earth was to give us the chance to play host to Him! As our permanent resident, the Spirit of Jesus can *keep alive* our wish for everything that has to do with God.

It is the work of that Spirit in us to guide us in hazard-free routes – avoiding the particular hazards which *He* sees as most dangerous. It's His work to whisper to us frequently about God's love, to make us really sure of it; it's His work to shine on our motivations and to remind us in times of temptation how priceless are the promises. It's the Jesus-in-us Who, at crucial moments, reminds us of our destiny, so that we'll reject things which are superficial or suspect.

*   *   *

Built-In Help

Prompting Us

We're going to get all sorts of surprises on our promise-journey . . . people (by no mere coincidence) will move into our path. Often, those people will have a faith which is weak or non-existent. Often those people will feel totally discouraged about life. It will be the Spirit of Jesus who will, so to speak, leap out from us to someone, and start that person hoping again.

It's worth remembering that the Spirit of Jesus can't leave us, even though we may often fail Him, as long as our desired destination remains the same. That destination has become very much *His* concern. This may seem a little foolish of Him, when we let Him down so much, but He knows what He's doing!

The world's complexities and our severe limitations may seem, at the level of our minds, to create terrific barriers to progress, but it is the loving activity of *Jesus* which guarantees our eventual arrival.

When we rather hesitatingly looked at a promise of God and felt that it might be for us, was God's Holy Spirit already in us? Yes, because it's through God's Spirit that a desire is put into us for everything which Jesus represents. Our unrecognized Guest was already making a way for a promise to come in at a deep level.

What keeps that spiritual desire-mechanism working in us is the Spirit of Jesus, even though we may frequently stray from the promise-road. In His love He desperately *wants* us to arrive.

When events almost force us to conclude that it is, after all, an uncaring universe, it's that gentle Spirit in us which says, "It may look uncaring, but it's not . . . and God's love means that all *must* come right for those who trust Him."

As far as humanly possible, promise-followers must ensure that the Spirit within us has lots and lots of freedom . . . that there's continuity of activity: Trust, blind trust, is a major ingredient of such a God-at-work situation.

The promised Holy Spirit is very much like an interior light in a world which doesn't always seem to make sense. Soon the presence of that light is demonstrated in our lives as we start, in an exciting way, to rise above our environmental limitations and personality limitations.

The promise of Jesus our Lord about the in-dwelling Spirit is well worth thinking about if we've a little time. Just think what a difference it makes if a life is Spirit-led and Spirit-powered. It goes far beyond just wearing the label "I'm charismatic".

As we think often of the Jesus-within, we can say, "Yes, Lord . . . please go on working". The work isn't always detected, but is very sure in its results!

* * *

PROMISES FOR TODAY

"The Holy Spirit helps us in our daily problems, and with our prayers."

Jesus tells us:

"The Kingdom of God is *within you*."

"The Holy Spirit, Who leads into all truth, will never leave you; He will take what is Mine, and make it known to you."

"The Father and I will make Our home within a person. . . ."

"Live in Me . . . and I in you!"

GRASPING THE PROMISES

Lord, thank You that Your presence with me is a constant one.

I make as my own Your promise to live in the hearts of Your children.

No matter what may be happening around me, I'll never forget that there are *two of us*! Thank You.

DAILY REMINDER NO.10

Thank You, Lord, that we're inseparable . . . and that nothing is impossible for me today.

13

Lots More Promises

No wonder that Jesus's early followers were so confident about passing on God's promises. . . . Their lives had just been permanently changed by one!

These men and women had experienced, in an intoxicating way, Jesus's promised gift (which we've just been considering) . . . the Holy Spirit. So elated were they by the experience, that drug-peddlars surely would have found no customers among them. Their elation had no "side-effects" . . . except a growing love for Jesus!

* * *

Most of the promises we have mentioned so far have been "direct quotes", you might say . . . God speaking straight at you and me. There are, of course, lots of other promises in the Bible, made by New Testament writers, which have been a terrific inspiration to people through the centuries.

* * *

Deeply-Felt

There was Paul! Paul didn't just write comforting words as he looked at the pleasant scene from his study window. Paul was the subject, not only of external pressures, but of intense inward struggle. As a result of all this, he became our expert in finding God in human suffering and conflict.

Writing with obvious divine authority, and with great warmth, Paul handed on to us lots of promises. . . .

> to those who, in this life, felt they had missed out. . . .

> to those who were afraid. . . .

> to those who felt beaten by circumstances. . . .

> to those who felt that God may have deserted them. . . .

> to those who just couldn't see a kind or understanding face anywhere.

* * *

Paul did more than any of Jesus's followers to help Christians to face disappointment and hardship in the right way . . . to set those things in their supernatural perspective. Listen to him now:

> "We can rejoice when we run into problems and trials, for we know that they are good for us."

"In all things God works for the good of those who love Him."

"Our sufferings bring patience; patience brings perseverance, and perseverance brings hope."

"We may be knocked down, but we are never knocked out."

"Through Him who loves us, we win an overwhelming victory."

"Our trials can teach us to rely, not on ourselves, but on God."

"If God is on our side who can ever be against us?"

"Whatever happens, be glad in the Lord."

"I am ready for anything through the strength of the One who lives within me."

* * *

As he looks to the future, shared with his beloved Jesus, Paul now feels moved to make some promises to you and me. It's as if, after looking at life's darker aspects, Paul is saying, "But I can promise you this. . . ." Listen!:

"Our light and momentary troubles are achieving for us an eternal glory which far outweighs them all."

That's a promise! . . .

"Although this outer man of ours may be falling into decay, the inner man is being renewed day by day. . . ."

And another! . . .

"Nothing can ever separate us from His love."

Another!

"We're one day going to stay with the Lord for ever!"

Another!

"By His power in us He can do infinitely more than we dare to ask or imagine."

Another!

"Certain of the glorious things He has for us in the future."

Another!

"When the time is ripe, He will gather us all together from wherever we are – in heaven or on earth – to be with God in Christ for ever."

Yet another!

* * *

Peter, who clearly has a different personality from that of Paul, nevertheless speaks in a remarkably similar way:

"Don't be surprised at the trials you're having to go through as Christians. . . ."

"The Lord can rescue us from all the temptations which surround us."

"The Lord is always thinking about you, and watching everything that concerns you."

"There's an inheritance which can't wear out . . . kept for you in heaven."

"God will open wide the gates of heaven for you to enter into the eternal Kingdom of our Lord and Saviour, Jesus Christ."

"A new heaven and a new earth, where there will be only goodness."

Jude is a less prominent New Testament writer, but in his very short letter he promises us that in all the ups and downs of life God can keep us from being permanently floored. After these ups and downs, says Jude, "God will present us before His glorious presence, without fault, and with great joy."

We can let John add his little bit:

"All you who believe in the name of Jesus, the Son of God, may be sure that you *have* eternal life."
"I can promise you that one day we'll see Him as He really is."

* * *

Twentieth-century followers of Jesus, coping with tremendous discouragements and real doubts from time to time, find that the words quoted here go right to the heart of what the life of a Christian is all about. It's good to take these words unhurriedly, day by day, and just receive them with the trusting, child-like simplicity which Jesus recommended. The Jesus-within will prompt us to say, with growing conviction, "Yes, Paul was dead right . . . so were Peter and the rest."

*　　*　　*

PROMISE FOR TODAY

Writes Paul:

"My God will supply all your need from His glorious riches in Christ Jesus."

GRASPING THE PROMISE

Dear Lord, so often I am confused about what I really need . . . my needs seem to change from day to day.

Thank You for Your promise that the meeting of my very deepest longings will present no problem to You.

I make Your promise mine right now – Thank You.

DAILY REMINDER NO. II

Lord Jesus, living in me, You are anticipating *all* today's needs. Thank You.

14

Choosing . . . Promise-Style

Do you find decisions easy?

When anyone asks that question, it often implies that they themselves don't. I must admit that I'm one of those who see certain issues as finely (and agonizingly!) balanced.

Are most of the world's problems caused by very decisive all-action people, who are never uncertain about anything? . . .

Or are those problems caused by those who dither, and neglect things which are crying out to be put right?

In either extreme (ultra-decisive or ultra-wobbly) great problems are caused . . . usually for *other* people, of course!

* * *

Promise-Illuminated

I believe that God has allowed the "uncertain" quality of our existence in order that our one great certainty, our one fixed place, might be found only in Himself.

It's interesting to find that every piece of bewilderment

about either our present or our future is "met" by one o
those promises. What the promises do is to set our lif
here in its true context . . . that we're just in one brie
stage of a well-planned long-term process.

Acceptance of God's promises ensures that the in
fluence of the long-term process is brought to bear on ou
present often complex affairs. The true perspective of the
entire creative scheme begins to influence the way we
choose to live each day. . . . We start to have a "promise
perspective".

Once certainty is found in the *spiritual* realm, when w
really see where life is leading, we find that even the mos
delicately balanced moral problems are illuminated fo
us.

There's no human problem which can't be solve
ultimately, if it is looked at in the light of God's promise
and tackled by promise-followers! That light gives in
spiration, it gives direction, and it sets free our mind
from the prejudice, the pettiness and the confusio
which causes us to fail.

After the calm contemplation of those promise
(especially, of course, one or two which we've made ou
own) we can usually find, in turning back to a specifi
situation, a sense of the path to follow, or find the ne
skill of patience (based on our certainty that He is work
ing for us).

In following the promises, so much is "decided" in
stinctively. . . . In other words, following a promis
means that many of the agonizing choices are by-passe
The choice just didn't arise, because with those promis
before us, an original error was avoided.

*   *   *

Changing Those Negatives

God's promises are there to be *set against* defeatism, or a lack of belief in oneself or in one's destiny. The promises are there to be set against the illusion that life is, after all, an empty and a meaningless exercise; there to be set against the old enemies of fear and guilt (which we'll be looking at in a little more detail shortly). Those promises are there to give that little "extra" when choosing what we know is right, against tremendous pressure.

The promises are there to be set against that feeling of being forsaken . . . there to occupy the painful void in us (created, perhaps, by other people's "depriving" or hurtful attitudes).

The promises are there to be set against the inclination to stand still, or even to go backwards, on our spiritual journey . . . they're there to push us forward, even when life has been cruel, and when all our will to continue has been lost.

We take that hesitant step forward because a promise of God in our heart gives just enough light to face the surrounding gloom, just enough sense of "future" to produce a little courage, so that we can press on again.

The promises exist to show us that life's "good luck" and "bad luck", and even its crippling disadvantages, are not important, compared with that marvellous *continuity* of a life shared with Jesus.

As we identify with the promises, we acquire that precious serenity of spirit which God wants each one of us to have.

A "child of promise" still has to come to terms with, or respond to, all sorts of anxiety-producing and disturbing factors. And yet he or she also manages, at the same time, a sense of walking above those disturbances. Ambidextrous (if you'll pardon the mixed metaphor).

The promise-journey is of a completely different order from the "normal" journey, in which people are affected so much by the world's deceptions, its obstacles, and its potential for destruction.

I wonder how many readers have reached the stage of being able to look at each one of those promises and see each as for them? Welcoming every promise means that *every* real need of ours which God sees is going to be met. Our life will have a sense of being surrounded by God's promises. If we're really centred on them, we'll be left, eventually, with only what is in those promises.

Don't forget that a resolute trust in God's promises *must* mean that gains are already being made in long-standing areas of weakness, so that we can thank God for that . . . right now!

* * *

PROMISES FOR TODAY

"God's blessings are received by faith . . . we are certain to get them, if we have faith like Abraham's!"

"All who trust in Jesus Christ receive the same blessing that Abraham received."

"Our certain hope will be like an anchor for us."

"We can completely count on God's promises, for it is impossible for Him to lie to us."

GRASPING THE PROMISES

Dear Lord, I will let the new perspective about life which the promises give affect my decision-making. I know that Your promises will help me to avoid the extremes of impulsiveness and dithering! Thank You for Your word about where "certainty" must lie for me. I make it mine now.

DAILY REMINDER NO. 12

Lord, thank You that nothing which today brings will outlast Your promises.

15

Both Kinds Are From Him!

"I had a strange sense of serenity and hope all through that recent trouble in the family."

"A friend sent me exactly enough to settle those debts. How he knew the amount I needed, I'll never know."

We hear promise-followers making statements like these quite frequently! It's never long before they realize that God has been at work in their circumstances. We are reminded that as part of His promise-keeping, God sends both spiritual and material help. We must be careful not to make an artificial distinction between the two.

* * *

One Whole

I'm sure that you've experienced, from time to time, the "arrival" of certain material supplies. These are needs which have not been specifically prayed about (though perhaps quietly wished for). And you've recognized, perhaps, that these things have come, with perfect timing, as part of God's provision.

If we make sure, always, that *spiritual* blessings are eagerly sought (especially the blessing of knowing Jesus), then such blessings will so often be accompanied by God's very definite meeting of current material needs. In fact, everything which we could possibly need is found somewhere in God's supply reserve . . . ready to be released in carrying out His promises to us.

Material things are not intrinsically bad, of course, although we all know how they can be terribly mis-used. God is able to see life's material things as part of His loving provision for those who trust Him . . . just as long as we don't fall into the trap of restricting our wishes to these things. (The wish for "results" in spiritual causes can get a bit like this!)

We find, in practice, that God's promised spiritual blessings so often include, also, something material which, in His love, He wishes us to have. Yes, God's promise-motivated provision for us is one whole. . . . He likes to include everything which can fulfil His intentions for us.

The way in which things happen in God's Kingdom is that when we seek something, absolutely abandoned to His will, the door opens for us to receive, in a surprisingly abundant way. It's as if we sense, on many occasions, God's enjoyment of our receiving a little better than we bargained for! If this abundant supply is not immediate, there's no cause to doubt God, or to be afraid, or to feel that we may have been mistaken about His promise-keeping. . . .

The translation of God's tremendous concern for us into provision (both spiritual and material), is a very sure

process. What we really need will come *when* it is
needed . . . and we'll know that it's from Him. He must
be absolutely trusted in this.

*   *   *

Let Them Come

How wonderfully we are able to say, when some need is
"surprisingly" met, "I didn't even make that a
priority. . . . All I did was to tell God that I trusted His
promises in a general sort of way."

We are going to see so many instances of material
provision as having been lovingly prepared . . . awaiting
our moment of need or our recognition of need. In
meeting the *real* needs of a promise-follower God may
seem to be "last-minute", but He's never too late!

If (being flesh and blood!) we're tempted to envy
others, let's remember that our standards are not
supposed to be the world's any more. When we
temporarily lack certain things (the "right" job, perhaps,
or deeply satisfying human friendships), this can never
be, in any way, a barrier to God's plans for us. The time
of lacking something, the time of waiting for certain
practical needs to be met, is one in which our spirits can
be enlarged, so to speak, in the things of God.

Just as God's "spiritual" answer is precisely what is
needed when we reach out in time of darkness, so His
meeting of some material needs is tied to His acute
awareness of all our circumstances.

Let us always be ready to receive "practical" gifts, or
offers of help (so often coming through the agency of

102

others who trust God). Let us see these things with God behind them, see them as necessity-awareness on the part of the Promise-Maker. We needn't feel a little ashamed when good things come, or help is offered. I'm sure that I've often hurt God by being a poor "taker". Don't let's be grudging receivers!

The one thing to be sure about is that we go on wanting, above all, Jesus's companionship . . . and wanting Him to be pleased with a growing harmony between His plans and ours.

* * *

PROMISES FOR TODAY

Jesus says:

"God will gladly give you all these things (such as food and clothing), if you give Him first place in your life."

"If, with all your imperfections, you try to give your own children what they really need, don't you realize that your heavenly Father will do at least as much?"

GRASPING THE PROMISES

Dear Lord, I accept that whatever I really need, materially, to get through this life will always come, if I trust You. I accept that Your spiritual blessings and Your material blessings are one whole.

Thank You for Your promise that as I go on wanting more of *You*, the "practical" things will come, as I need them.

I take a firm hold of that promise now.

DAILY REMINDER NO. 13

Thank You, Lord, that when I reach a place of need today, Your supply will be there for me.

16

Refusing The Lie

"Look, Susan . . . God loves you. He thinks the world of you. He'll always forgive you."

"Yes, but you don't know what a terrible person I really am. I'm sure I deserve only bad things to happen to me."

* * *

Resistance

The sort of conversation quoted above is always happening, and illustrates the fact that nowhere are God's loving promises more fiercely contested than in the area of guilt and despair.

Over and over again you find well-intentioned God-hungry people with a general feeling of shame . . . an "undeserving" sense. You're aware of tremendous resistance when you tell them how much God loves them, and wants to welcome them back after failure.

When you've listened many times to sad people whose lives are being paralysed with guilt, you begin to realize that this is no mere bio-chemical reaction, resulting in an inability to forgive oneself. You realize that God's love is actually being *opposed* . . . opposed by a spiritual force which, though intangible, is very real.

The more you encounter this sort of situation the more you realize that the *only* solution to a "spiritual problem" is a spiritual one. God's love-promises desperately need to find a place deep inside that tortured person.

Those who have tried to follow Jesus for some time discover that to describe supernatural evil as a "tempting agency" is totally inadequate! Evil influences have, in fact, a dual role. . . . That dual role is one of tempting us . . . and then paralysing us with guilt about precisely the action into which they pushed us! We must learn to distinguish between the healthy conscience, which "represents" God's disapproval, and a tortured and prolonged state of guilt.

All this would, of course, sound a little unreal and even melodramatic to, say, a non-believing psychiatrist. But in fact I have seen the guilt-prison unlocked many, many times, by the spiritual answer . . . when other ways have proved inadequate.

* * *

Refusing To Listen

To doubt God's basic, and "almost foolish" forgiving nature will be a strong temptation at many places on the promise-road.

Those who have completed their spiritual journey through this world have had to cling, fiercely at times, to that basic nature of God. Clinging, when pressure to

oubt that divine nature was tremendous. . . . Con-
dence in God had to be coupled with a resolute refusal
listen to accusations inspired by forces which are God's
elentless enemy.

Obviously, a sense of shame about failures can be a
ealthy thing, and a constructive one. Seeing wrong
ings as God does, and hating them, removes all sorts of
mporary barriers and leads to a restored relationship
ith Him. But a continuing self-blame is entirely
ifferent, and must never be allowed to check our pro-
ress towards realizing God's promises and our partial
njoyment of those promises now.

Nowhere is that natural "spilling over" of trust in the
romises into trust in God's own *Person* so important as
this sphere of paralysing guilt.

So fierce can be the blame-sense at times that God's
romises and assurances about His forgiving nature –
learly and frequently given – may seem to lose their
ower. . . .

. . . We may be lured into taking over God's own
ole . . . judging ourselves. When this becomes ex-
ggerated, all sorts of self-punishing devices are indulged
1. This can happen, of course, even after we've earnestly
ought, and received, God's forgiveness about some-
ing. In an oppressive state of self-blame, we may find it
ard, for the moment, to think of a promise which will fit
e situation. It is then that we'll turn, helplessly
erhaps, to the *Person* and to His love. . . .

We can be absolutely sure that it is hurting God when
e go on living under that cloud of guilt (failing, for
arious reasons, to enjoy the full impact of His love). . . .

In face of all this, what did Jesus say? **He said we
hould cheer up!**

Evil's guilt-producing influence may be strong, bu
even stronger, if only we'll turn to it, is another influence
We must *never* believe the lie that those source areas c
self-blame can't be reached. They can. We are not des
tined to live with a self-condemning personality, . .
especially if we're "promise-children"!

* * *

Keeping Our Momentum

Remember that child-like, but rather determined belief i
God's promises which first motivated us to accept some o
them? Well, that same determined belief can come to ou
rescue in conquering the insidious influence of "th
accuser of Christians" (as the Bible describes evil).

We've got to tell ourselves repeatedly (and thank Hir
for the fact), that God's mercy sweeps away all thos
occasions of letting Him down. Those imprisoned area
where we usually find both doubt of God and doubt o
ourselves can be unlocked. Those areas are unlocked a
we see all the wonderful promises of God's tender lo
summed up in . . . Himself. Although God does not wa
us to be blind to our failings, He's even more hurt if v
become paralysed. . . .

He wants to save us from that failure to trust in H
love . . . (or perhaps more accurately, a failure of *a
termination* to trust).

"Lord, You've swept it all away. Thank You! A
You're cleansing out all the guilt-feelings. Tha
You!"

Affirmations like this about God's forgiving nature (no matter how we may be feeling), are all that He needs to ensure that the momentum of our promise-journey isn't lost.

A promise-follower must always take sides with God's love against the accusations of evil – posing, as it often does, as "God's moral voice". Progress on the promise-road is based on the absolute unchangeability of God's nature . . . it is based on our perception that persistent and devastating guilt is a *lie*.

If we slip badly on our promise-inspired journey, let's remember that on all those occasions of failure, God gives us instant access to the quiet of His presence. Don't let's waste a second in entering that welcoming presence, however ashamed, however disgusted with ourselves.

There, in His presence, we'll listen to no other voice but that of His love. . . . His love will not be minimizing what we've done, not "excusing" it, but most definitely *welcoming back* (perhaps for the hundredth time this week!), if we are truly sorry.

Some people, more than others, are inclined to blame themselves, of course. But even the most "scrupulous" of people have it in us to make a very simple, basic choice. That choice is just to bank on God's merciful promises. Staking everything on His loving and understanding nature, we'll be amazed at how we are shielded from that accusing voice along the promise-road.

To some, all this may appear to be creating our own "sloppy" God. But, in fact, a person who draws heavily on God's mercy eventually becomes a much better person. . . . In making His love-promises, God knows what He's doing!

PROMISES FOR TODAY

"I, your Lord, will both forgive . . . and forget."

"You can be of good cheer; your sins are forgiven."

(There are lots more like these!)

GRASPING THE PROMISES

Dear Lord, I see the desperate need to let Your love permeate those areas deep within where an "undeserving" sense may be lurking.

I also believe that if I resolutely trust Your promise here, Your love is going to break down those guilt-barriers.

I take a firm hold of Your promise now.

I will refuse to be burdened, knowing that not only do You forgive, but forget . . . those failures no longer exist in Your sight. Thank You.

DAILY REMINDER NO. 14

Lord, thank You that Your love is freeing me from needless guilt.

17

A Little Anticipation!

I'm sure that you've been on a holiday which turned out to be completely over-rated. You were glad to get home! And yet, the disappointing holiday could not take away the months of pleasurable anticipation under the spell of beautifully-illustrated guide books and travel brochures.

A sure way to create a virtually unshakeable promise-sense in us, is to develop an *anticipatory gratitude*. We need to thank God every day (in the midst of all our promises), in anticipation of His promises. We need to thank Him, too, for the fact that we are *currently receiving* as a result of those promises.

The gratitude habit is one of the reasons why the various daily "thank-You" reminders are included in our book. There should be days when we can get through all the "reminders" at odd moments (they're very short!) Anyway, the important thing is that no day should go by without some expression of gratitude for the promises which are now ours. . . . Our gratitude will, of course, bring promise-realization closer.

* * *

Our thanksgiving for the promises shows God that our life is now being lived on the basis of His dependability. We're wise to see God's promises as in a *continuous daily process* of being realized. We can then express our grateful recognition of this fact. A sense of gratitude and a sense of "receiving" (because of promise-acceptance) are inseparable.

A *regular* thank-You to God for what He has got planned for us can wonderfully deepen the promise-sense. Our "thank-You" can help us to feel a link with those great characters mentioned earlier, who ignored their circumstances and said such extravagant and joyful things about God! This deepening promise-sense will no longer depend on what life brings to us . . . and it need not depend on our variable awareness of God. True thanksgiving will become habitual if we resolutely refuse all thoughts which are not "promise-trusting" ones. Doubt holds up realization.

Obviously, it's better if our thanks to God for His promises ("our" promises, if you prefer), are set against life's various misfortunes *as soon as they arise*. Never is an expression of gratitude for God's promises more powerful than in the context of temporary doubt or disappointment. Our continued gratitude in such a context can mean that it's not usually very long before there's some sign that God hasn't forgotten us. It's not usually very long before we experience what seems like a Divine "response" to our anticipatory gratitude. The "promise-sense" will have become part of our very being, just like the blood circulating in us.

It's as if our gratitude anticipates that eventual meeting

place with God . . . at which we've been moved towards His promises and they have been moving towards us!

* * *

Sampled Now

Regularly thanking God for His promises is one vital aspect of our "general" gratitude for the fact of Himself, and for His sharing in our earthly existence.

God's unfailing response to things like trust, and appreciation, becomes an increasingly familiar thing if we're Jesus's followers. If we're living in that state of anticipation (based on confidence in Jesus as our Dependable Companion), we will never end up disappointed. **There's so much waiting for us . . . what our thanksgiving does is to release a little of it!**

Our thanks make it possible for our current situation to be flooded with a sense of God's generosity and love.

Imagine God's joy in cases where He doesn't have to withhold from us (for, say, sixty or seventy years) the experience of promise-realization! Instead, because of His love, God can shower upon His grateful children things which belong to the spirit realm . . . things to be "sampled" now before our earthly existence is left behind.

As part of His promises to us God is sure to grant those very deepest desires of our hearts (so difficult to put into words). Let us thank Him for this, and begin to experience the process a little . . . even in the most unfavourable conditions.

"Thank You, Lord, that everything which You have planned for me *will* happen. . . ."

"Thank You that Your promises *are* working out. . . ."

*　*　*

Anticipation is a marvellous thing, isn't it?

People don't always realize the *peace* which comes to a believing person from anticipation of God's loving purposes. That growing certainty of eventual joy in the presence of Jesus means peace in our hearts, *now*, as we move towards that joy. And we know that (unlike that disastrous holiday) our anticipation of what God has planned for us will turn out to have been fully justified.

Whenever we spare a moment or two to thank God for His love let's thank Him, too, for all that that love *is creating* for us in early promise-realization.

*　*　*

PROMISE FOR TODAY

"If you pray with thanksgiving, you will surely experience God's peace."

GRASPING THE PROMISE

Dear Lord, help me to show that Your promises live in me, by regularly thanking You for them.

Let my gratitude deepen that sense of anticipation, concerning all that You have planned for me.

I accept with all my heart Your promise here of peace . . . inseparable from gratitude.

DAILY REMINDER NO. 15

Lord, thank You for all Your promises, and for all that I am receiving from You today.

Here and there, in the remainder of the book, are quoted examples of the things frequently said by troubled people. There are sure to be times when we can identify with many of these comments, or with the feelings expressed.

We can always find a promise of God to apply to a situation, or to suit any temperament. And so, here are some of those promises, and words of encouragement, to keep by us and use as various needs arise.

Most of the following verses are borrowed from *The Living Bible* and are gratefully acknowledged. One or two are my own rather bold paraphrases! . . .

THINGS THEY SAY

"When I contemplate the future, I can't help being filled with apprehension."

* * *

The Answer

"Don't worry about anything whatsoever. Tell God your needs . . . and you will know His peace, which is far more wonderful than the human mind can understand."

Jesus's promise:

"*God* will take care of your tomorrow. You can live one day at a time!"

* * *

THINGS THEY SAY

"Some people seem even more unreasonable, even more hostile, when they know I'm a Christian!"

* * *

Jesus says:

"When you are persecuted and lied about because you are My follower . . . wonderful! Be happy about it . . . for a tremendous reward awaits you in heaven. . . .

"Since they persecuted Me, naturally they will persecute you!"

* * *

St Paul says:

"If God is for us, who can ever be against us?"

* * *

THINGS THEY SAY

"Does God really care for individuals like myself who are always failing? Is His love more 'general' than 'personal'?"

*   *   *

The Answer:

"God knows the number of hairs on your head!"

"He will not let your foot slip."

"He will defend *each one* who comes to Him for protection."

*   *   *

His Word:

"I have called you by name. You are *Mine*!"

*   *   *

THINGS THEY SAY

"There are one or two temptations which usually prove too strong for me."

* * *

The Answer:

"We must never forget that *God has already rescued us from the power of darkness.*"

"God will not let you be tempted beyond your strength. . . ."

* * *

God's Promises:

"I will uphold you with My victorious right hand."

"Don't be afraid. I am here to help you."

* * *

18

God's Achievers

"Anything is possible for you". . . .

Here's Jesus, telling us what we can expect if we live
the life of faith, and if we let Him live in us, and transform us.

* * *

Most of us have had dreams of being among the world's
great "achievers" . . . also, no doubt, of being among the
world's great Christians! Sadly, perhaps, the achievements
have eventually been consigned to the dustbin of fantasy.
We dreamt of achieving, but, after experiencing some
harsh realities, may have settled for a compromise.

We must remember that the things which God sees as
achievements can't always be measured by the standards
which are usually adopted. This is why it's no false
encouragement for those starting to live by God's promises to say that they could be becoming great achievers
without realizing it! Even in the early stages of our belief
that God is going to do great things, we find that we're
starting to be *used*.

For example, as we start to live by God's promises,
there can be a quiet but decisive turn-round in the life of

a friend, or other contact of ours. As we keep our eyes on our own very special promise or promises, someone may receive a real "injection" of faith, after talking with us.

That increasingly permanent sense of hope which comes from our acceptance of what God has promised will begin to rub off on to other people. These people will detect that we're travelling along a purposeful route. God, in His own unique way, will make sure that a contact of ours starts to feel hope, even if we feel that we've made no "significant" comments.

The recipients won't always register instant recognition and thank us, of course, but God has seen it all and knows that He *used* us. He used our concern, used our kind words, used our good-listener role. "Nothing you do for the Lord is ever wasted", said Paul. If we simply accept the fact of God's existence, and the *reality* of what He has promised, we're bound to be making some impact on the surrounding spiritual darkness.

* * *

Keeping It Real

What is real achievement in God's scheme of things?

I'm sure that such achievement happens when there's a permanent change within the nature of a person. The change has nothing to do with putting on the religious style, or feeling that one has arrived as a "Christian personality" (ugh!) It hasn't anything to do with smug counting up of "results" in Christian work!

I am convinced that there is an important word of warning to all of us who may want to be Christian achievers: **Don't be lured into pouring energy into things which may bring rapid and tangible results or "feed-backs", or men's praise, if it means breaking off the deeper work which God can do through you**.

It's obvious that all real achievements have to be lasting. A perfect example of this is when one of us who is a promise-follower is responsible (perhaps by a word we have spoken or simply by our life-style), for someone else grasping a promise! This achievement becomes one of eternal significance. We have become like one of those branches with lots of grapes on them because promise-acceptance has brought about the closeness of Jesus.

Is our existence very restricted, a little humdrum? Or is our existence tremendously varied, and almost too challenging at times? The environment really doesn't matter, because if we've grasped a few of God's promises, and they're affecting our lives, He is sure to be using us to reduce the world's unbelief and unhappiness.

* * *

Winning Influence

How can we describe what's going on in a promise-based life?

Well, not only is our spirit developing in its true direction, but there's a very real influence of love from that life! (Paul said that we become like mirrors reflecting God's glory.) It's for this reason that we must never, even slightly, undervalue the achievements of a day lived in God's company, believing in, and thanking Him for, His promises.

As we try to negotiate the promise-road what else is God up to?

In the first place, of course, He is *guiding*. There's a gentle but inexorable drawing to Himself. Then there's considerable *activity* . . . sending love, through us, into places where there used to be mistrust and fear. ("You'll be given the right words", was one of His promises.)

This activity of love through one "ordinary" human life is part of what will be the eventual triumph of God's love over everything in this universe which opposes it. "God has given you the whole world to use!" said Paul.

When we start to put our trust in God's promises, it's as if He challenges us: "Now, do you want to be a *real* achiever, not just a superficial one?" If this is our ambition, He's going to give us many achievement-impulses to follow each day.

Do some aspects of life seem anything but achievement right now? Well, if Jesus and those promises are ours (possibly still in the early slightly trembling stages), we must *not* accept the "appearance" of non-achievement. We may not see much of the "fruit" which Jesus is producing just yet, but we'll certainly see it later.

We talked earlier about how mountains are moved by certain remarkable people. Well, they're really not so remarkable are they? . . .

Tremendous obstacles are being moved all the time by modest people who, over-awed by the size of those obstacles, then call in the Expert!

* * *

PROMISES FOR TODAY

I'm sure that Abraham wouldn't mind, once again, if we promise-followers borrowed something which God said to him . . . with one eye on us of course!

"You are going to be a blessing to many others."

GRASPING THE PROMISES

Lord, I only want to bask in achievements which *You* see as such . . . the rest don't matter!

And I'll never forget that it's always *Your* influence which counts . . .

Thank You for Your word, here, that someone who follows Your promises will be a blessing to other people. I don't want this promise to be in the category of nice sounding words any more. I'm going to take the "blessing to others" process for granted from now on. Thank You.

DAILY REMINDER NO. 16

"Dear Lord Jesus, thank You that You're not wasting me today."

THINGS THEY SAY

"When I look at some other Christians, and then at my own weaknesses and frequent failures, I wonder whether spiritual life really is for me."

*　　*　　*

His Answer:

"Happy are those who *know* their need of God, for the Kingdom of Heaven is theirs!"

"Do not be dismayed. I am your God, and I strengthen you."

"Keep knocking . . . and the door *will* be opened to you."

*　　*　　*

THINGS THEY SAY

"On some days I can hardly make the effort to pray. I have the time, but not the inclination."

* * *

The Answer:

"Don't be weary in prayer. Keep at it. Watch for God's answers."

"The nearer you go to God, the nearer He will come to you."

Jesus says:

"Apart from Me, you can't do a thing."

* * *

THINGS THEY SAY

"How can I bear, much longer, this awful sense of emptiness? It's hard to believe, at times, that a loved one has gone to be in God's care."

* * *

Jesus promises:

"In my Father's house are many rooms. . . ."

"Happy are those who mourn now for they shall be comforted."

"Your sorrow will be turned into a wonderful joy. . . . No one shall rob you of that joy."

* * *

19

Obstacles Into Miracles

God sees our world (we can always think of ways in which we could have planned it better!) as a vital step towards the full realization of our spirit-potential.

Keats, of course, put it more neatly than I've just done when he simply called this world "the vale of soul-making".

* * *

Carried

In a puzzling existence like ours it's obvious that in pursuing God's promises we'll be tempted to become disillusioned, or to give up completely. At the end of this chapter is printed a very familiar verse about what is being prepared in the spiritual sphere. But on our journey to that sphere we'll become aware of fierce conflicts – especially reserved, it often seems, for Jesus's followers!

That's the negative side; but with a promise of God before us, we'll also find a remarkable sense of being *carried* along that road. It's as if we become increasingly immune from the more permanent results of the shattering reverses (the road blocks), which threatened to check our progress.

It's hard to explain unless you've experienced it, but there's a definite sense of God literally taking us over so many danger factors.

Obviously we won't always feel God's companionship warmly, but deep inside we'll simply take it for granted that He's with us. We'll realize that the often surprising confidence with which we start to meet the challenges of each day is one proof of His closeness.

Our new and purposeful promise-road isn't easy, but in the things which are important, it's a completely safe road. Possibly, in travelling this road, we may have to give up one or two things to which we've clung, but this won't cause us any real regrets. . . . Possessing our Companion will more than make up for those things.

As we mentioned a short time ago, the various "chance-events" can be seen in a new perspective, can be seen in relation to the promises. In fact, many of the "coincidental" happenings will now be experienced as actually helping along what God has promised to us.

*   *   *

Transformed

As we cling to a Divine promise we find some of life's harsh realities are bringing that promise a little closer! There are times, as we know, when life's almost unbearable misfortunes look like totally eclipsing all our But if we have, at some stage, warmly received

God's promises it's as if there is always a faint glow around the edges of that temporary eclipse. That continuing light, though perhaps only just discernible, shows us that the eclipse of hope is not really total, and certainly not permanent.

The memory of a promise "made ours" will so often blunt the cutting edge of what could have been devastating. . . . When the great shock of these "devastating" events has subsided a little, we may begin to see them as fitting into God's strategy for us – even though we may still dearly wish that they had never happened. In the shock of some events, as we know, God can show us truths only partially seen beforehand, and deepen our trust towards Him. He may be doing that, right now, with someone reading this.

It's only when we are keeping a promise of God as our goal that we can sense Him making what would otherwise be futile or wasteful into steps of a spiritual ladder. Seeing this, we're not going to be swept off our feet by life's fluctuations.

Obviously non-believers, including some lovable idealists and humanists, would never see things in this way, but promise-followers become increasingly aware of the way in which God wonderfully handles life's basic material . . . turning obstacles into miracles.

Jesus is the place where God's promises *live*. It's no mere platitude to say that if we're firmly focused on Jesus there can be an uncanny transformation of the difficult places and a wonderful using of obstacles.

At times of great uncertainty, it can help to know that at least we're lost on *His* road!

* * *

Inseparable

In following the promise-road we don't envy those "real Christians" any longer. We realize that whatever it was that we had previously, it wasn't the real life, the life of hope, which acceptance of God's promises has brought.

It's along the promise-road that we will instinctively turn to our Companion and draw from Him in all sorts of details – knowing that He enjoys being drawn upon!

Clearly we are not going to be in a constant state of euphoria on this journey. We won't be blissfully unaware of life's darker side . . . in fact there's likely to be an increased awareness of it. We'll almost certainly know loneliness, possibly hostility, and complete misunderstanding. But these things will only show up more vividly what God has promised us.

Ideally, along with the great saints, we'll learn not to look too much at the tough nature of the promise-road, but at the Promise-Maker Himself. The place towards which we're heading is simply to be with Jesus in that realm of realization, where we shall have no regrets about what we've "missed" here.

A sure sign that we're still on the promise-road is when we want more and more of Jesus! It's a sure sign when our motivation is not fear, but a wonderful sense of gratitude for what He is doing.

Miracles – large and "small" – are sure to be happening in us on the promise-journey. Even if we're shy, or not very eloquent, it's probable that we'll find ourselves quietly telling one or two others about the very dependable Friend who accompanies us. By the way, how much stronger are these shy little "testimonies" than some of the powerful, one-eye-on-the-audience type!

The great thing about the promise-based life is that when things go terribly wrong, there's always the *inseparability* of our Companion to fall back upon.

Because the promise-road is essentially an upward one, we'll find that many of the holds which evil forces used to have on us have, so to speak, dropped away further back. On the promise-road, our Companion will help us to change those darker moods of ours as no other agency can. With His promises firmly before us we'll be increasingly serene, controlled, forgiving, patient, and almost reckless in some previously timid areas!

And so, without losing our realism about life, we find that the promises which we've made our own bring an incredible optimism . . . one which infiltrates our current circumstances.

* * *

A PROMISE FOR TODAY

Jesus says:

"I am going away to prepare for your coming, so that You can always be *with Me* where I am."

"With Me . . ."

"With Me . . ."

"With Me . . ."

GRASPING THE PROMISE

Dear Lord, I let Your words "with Me" echo deep inside me. I take a firm grasp on Your promise that You will bring me, one day, to be with You in the fullest possible sense.

I know that Your promise is going to be a source of steadiness when life threatens to become chaotic. Thank You.

DAILY REMINDER NO. 17

Lord Jesus, thank You for the place which, right now, You are preparing for me.

THINGS THEY SAY

"I'm a believer, but I can't help envying some people's affluence and success!"

* * *

The Answer:

"**The Lord Himself** will be your inheritance."

* * *

God says:

"Anyone who loves and follows *Me* is indeed wealthy."

"What profit is there even if you gain the whole world and fail to attain eternal life?"

* * *

St Paul wrote:

"I look upon everything as loss, compared with the overwhelming gain of knowing Jesus my Lord."

* * *

THINGS THEY SAY

"I live in a state of feeling that something terrible is about to happen to me."

*   *   *

The Answer:

"The eternal God is your refuge. Underneath are His everlasting arms."

"He protects you day and night. He will keep you from all evil, and preserve your life."

"To trust in God means complete safety."

"Let Him have *all* your worries and cares."

*   *   *

THINGS THEY SAY

"It's sometimes hard to be sure that I'm really forgiven."

* * *

The Answer:

"There will be no condemnation awaiting those who belong to Christ Jesus our Lord."

"Everyone who trusts in Him will be *freed* from guilt."

God's promise:

"I will cleanse away *all* your sins. . . ."

* * *

20

Fear Meets Its Match!

Irrational fear, that dread of consequences which don't, in fact, occur, is widespread.

Irrational fear lies behind so many of our bad relationships, and our faulty decision-making. Because this sort of fear is based on a lie, you won't be surprised at my conclusion that it originates in those evil forces, trying consistently to wreck God's purposes.

Fear (when, so often, there is logically nothing to fear) becomes habitual. Such fear is both God's enemy and ours, of course. *God, in fact, gave His promises as a direct opposing force to the widespread fears of mankind.* Once we start to live by those promises, they can miraculously change even the most fear-burdened life.

The promises exist to meet so many kinds of need. Their presence in our thinking processes means that our emotions, our passions, our misgivings and our fears *can* be kept strictly controlled . . . unable to deflect God's unique plan for our life.

* * *

Fear Meets Its Match!

Striking at The Fear-Source

We have seen that God's promises always have in them a love-message, and something to start us hoping again. The more warmly the promises have been received, the less room there is going to be for fear.

Fear (sometimes of everything) may have become almost a way of life, but one of the many results of starting to trust God's promises is that we find a new outlook, a new way of meeting each day. Trusting those promises, each new day is no longer a thing to be "faced".

The promises cause optimism to peep out from a previously down-turned disposition . . . and fear recedes a little. Then, a courage which we never knew peeps out . . . and fear recedes a little further! Behind each promise it's as if we see a sort of "glow", which is God's love . . . an all-enveloping love. To quote John, the New Testament writer, love has the characteristic of driving out fear, even if it has become well established in a person's nature.

The ultimate fear, of course, is that of extinction; knowing this, God has provided promises to act as a shield against bitter despair. If we can warmly embrace the end-result towards which the promise is directed, this takes away our fear. As so many have found, it happens in the most daunting circumstances.

There's always a tendency for fear to creep up on us if there's a sense of love being absent from our life. Even the input of human love succeeds only in minimizing, to some extent, the fear in a person's heart.

It is the *Divine* love, coming uniquely through God's encouraging words of promise, which actually strikes at the deepest roots of fear. These words (much more dynamic than the temporary uplift of "something we have read" or "something someone said to us"), create a quiet, patient optimism which can stand up against life's "disadvantages".

* * *

Gambling On The Promises

And so, what can we do when we find that we've slipped into a state of fear?

Recognizing it, we must oppose the fear by selecting one of "our" promises and *standing very firmly on it* (as the old hymns used to say). The promise will in fact convey the *presence* . . . and it's that presence which now gives us the strength to start acting contrary to the fear-state.

If only more Christians could see that circumstances can be robbed of their fear-potential when a promise of God (looking beyond the threatened consequences), is firmly held!

During the "average" day fear can become the dominant emotion for much of the time. When we feel this state of fear coming on, there couldn't be a better moment for us to state (aloud, if necessary) our trust in God's promises . . . (e.g. "Lord, in You, I have nothing to fear"). At that moment, there's a closer uniting of ourselves with God as He involves Himself more deeply in our current situation.

This state of unity, which comes naturally from holding to a promise, has the power to sweep away the ground from under the feet of fear! *God wants us, in life's frightening places, instinctively to transfer the future tense of a promise into a present one*. . . . "**This** is the moment when God said He'd be with me and strengthen me!"

God wants all of His "promise-children" to move out of the sphere of self-deception into that of truth . . .

When those fears, implanted by evil, turn out to have been without foundation (having in so many cases ruined our lives), we shall realize that the promises of God were the voice of truth, all along . . . if only we had listened. It's better not to wait for that moment of truth, however! We must gamble *now* on God's promises being absolutely true, and our irrational fears (including paranoid fears of other people), absolute deception.

Let us waste no further time before building from those loving promises of God, a kind of fortress against every kind of fear . . . which is *exactly* what He intended His promises to be.

*   *   *

PROMISES FOR TODAY

"Don't be fearful . . . I will defend you, and I will give you great blessings."

"So don't be afraid, little flock. It gives your Father great happiness to give you the Kingdom."

GRASPING THE PROMISES

Dear Lord, I am going to let fear be a thing of the past. I'm going to allow Your promises to burn more deeply than ever before.

I see the importance of simply refusing to be afraid and standing on a promise instead.

I make Your promises here of blessing (and of entry into Your Kingdom) my own, right now.

DAILY REMINDER NO. 18

Lord, thank You that I will always be within Your love, and need have no fear this day.

THINGS THEY SAY

"I dread each night. . . ."

* * *

The Answer:

"In Me, you will lie down in peace and safety, un-afraid."

"His peace will keep your thoughts and your hearts quiet, and at rest, as you trust in Christ Jesus."

Jesus says:

"Do not let your heart be troubled. . . . My peace I give to You."

"Come to Me. . . . I will give you rest for your soul."

* * *

THINGS THEY SAY

"Just at the moment there seems no one I really can trust . . . no one to lean upon."

* * *

The Answer:

"Give all your burdens to the Lord. *He* will carry them."

"The Lord will watch over your comings and goings . . . both now and for evermore."

* * *

Jesus says:

"I am the Good Shepherd . . . I will never turn away anyone who comes to Me."

* * *

THINGS THEY SAY

"To face a new day is almost impossible."

* * *

The Answer:

"Be unafraid, be confident . . . for wherever you go, the Lord is with you."

"Commit your way to the Lord. Trust in Him, and He will act for you."

"When you suffer, or are tempted, He is wonderfully able to help you."

"In God is your everlasting strength."

* * *

21

Confident!

I'm not too fond of the phrase "prayer-times", are you?
It's a bit like switching on God for a few minutes, and
then returning to reality!

Hopefully we've developed, as "promise-graspers", a
fairly constant sense (varying in intensity, of course), of
God's presence. Our life can now be revolutionized, if we
will always remember two things:

> God would not have promised what He didn't want
> us to have.

> God would not have promised what He felt we
> would probably fail to achieve.

*   *   *

"Purified" Requests

Once we get that warm feeling about the dependability of
God's promises, the most natural response is to ask,
"Now, Lord, what can I do to help along Your pro-
mises?" Often, of course, the answer is "Nothing!"

God's intervention, as we know, can be completely independent of our own contribution – yes, even independent of our own right or "positive" attitude. In other words, God sometimes takes by the scruff of the neck circumstances over which we have no possible control, and makes them come into line with His promises for us.

But at other times, when we ask, "Lord, what can I do to help the process?", God seems to whisper, "Yes, you *can* hasten the achievement of what I have promised. You *can* play a part in bringing those deep desires of your heart a little closer."

Our desires! Don't they need a very careful examination at times? Don't you sometimes feel that the whole lot need to be put into a sort of spiritual washing-machine?

We are wise, when pursuing God's promises, to submit all our ambitions and wishes ("spiritual" ones included!) to this cleaning process. As we do so, we must want to see, as He does, what is really worth striving for; we must want our wishes to start coinciding with His.

God seems to have so arranged that when our various desires have been through this cleansing or screening process our prayer-requests start to be answered ones. It's not long before we see clearly the things which can be ours, the things which we can confidently ask.

A typical "purified request", for example, is "Lord, let me live more closely to You". This one invariably seems to bring an automatic response! There are many, many others which God will show to us.

* * *

Optimism

The combination of (1) submitting desires to the screening process, and (2) our acceptance of God's promises, will begin to make almost anything possible for us.

If we're allowing God's loving and gentle control, and we've left behind, in the dirty water, all the resentments and wrong objectives, those words of Jesus, "Ask anything you like", which once seemed too good to be true, begin to have an exciting new meaning. It's as if we become aware of Jesus our Lord giving us a nudge in our quiet moments: "Go on, John . . . Go on, Susan . . . *ask* Me for that. I want you to have it."

In the same way we seem to sense God nudging us with "I'd like you to think about Jane. I would particularly like to use a prayer of yours for *her*."

As God "gives" these people to us, it's usually accompanied by an optimism which we don't always feel when praying in church about "the people in Central Africa" or "the coming election".

*   *   *

Promise-Inspired

Over and over again, we find that God's wonderful shaping of events is out of all proportion to the simple two-minute prayer about which He prompted us.

As we get some of our desires and objectives right, we find that those God-prompted things upon which we act have inevitable, and often uncanny, consequences. We can almost sense God putting into motion forces to bring about that for which we've prayed, in a way not previously experienced.

We also begin to feel God's *delight* in our asking, and His delight in sending what is best for us, or for a friend. We won't now feel that our demands might have become a little unreasonable!

As God and we become more closely involved in each other, our prayers will begin to seem all like a simple promise-*acceptance*. At the heart of our prayers is an acceptance that there is no limit to what God can bring about. If someone overheard our "purified" and God-prompted prayers, he or she would probably think, "That person seems to believe that God can do *anything!*"

The eavesdropper on our prayers would probably be thinking as well, "What a lot of thank-You's!" Yes, in promise-inspired prayers, "thank You" passes from a duty into an instinct, we begin taking for granted that God will give us what we really need. We take for granted that God can't fail to respond to the prayer of a promise-follower, about which He has given that "nudge".

On the promise-road, of course, we'll often experience a sense of God's *anticipation* of our prayer-requests . . . "The Lord knew I'd be needing that . . . I didn't even have to ask!"

* * *

Recognition

To be realistic, realized promises and answered prayers do take varying amounts of time! What really matters, of course, is not the time-scale, but the sureness of the *result*. We can trust in the Lord's unerring timing about all our prayer-requests.

What a difference it now makes in our conversations with God if we have that growing certainty, in spite of all current evidence, that His promises are on their way to us. It is not self-deception to say with all our heart, "He *is* answering my prayers, and I know that I will detect the process, increasingly."

After making purified and promise-based requests we can even look up from some of our discouraging or slow-changing circumstances and, with a leap of faith, say "That's right, Lord. Keep up the good work!"

By the way, what a lot of power there is in those trusting little arrow-prayers. . . .

It's as if we now begin to climb into God's skin when we are praying and start to acquire His viewpoint that, in fact, nothing can frustrate His plans for us. Those plans are perfect, of course, and He is determined that one day that same adjective can be applied to us!

* * *

Along our promise-road we'll sense that the Maker of the promises is somehow bringing everything into a wonderful harmony for us. As Paul said, God can bring about far more than we even dare to ask or imagine, in our wildest dreams.

As we learn, instinctively, to give life's crises into our wonderful Lord's hands (with His *dependency* very firmly in mind), we are bound to experience Him stepping in, often in remarkable ways. For example, we'll be told that God has started to bring healing into a situation which we brought to Him, perhaps only minutes ago. We'll *know* that there is an anxiety-reduction on giving to Him a hurt-feeling situation, or on mentioning that person who seems determined to ruin everything we stand for. That anxiety-reduction is based (even if we're not analysing it as such at the time) on our acceptance of God's promises to us.

Our "Mr Reliable" (if that still isn't too jarring a title for Him!) gives us that upsurge of peace, that sense of spirit-healing, as we now give things *confidently* to Him.

* * *

PROMISES FOR TODAY

Jesus says:

"Ask . . . and you will receive."

"Search . . . and you will find."

"Knock . . . and the door will open."

"Ask and receive, so that your joy may be full."

GRASPING THE PROMISES

Dear Lord, help me fearlessly to look with You at my desires and ambitions.

I completely accept Your promise that Your Spirit in me will show me all the things for which I can confidently ask.

I accept that Your promise to those who ask and search is not too good to be true! I gladly make that promise mine now.

DAILY REMINDER NO. 19

Lord, thank You that during today You are answering my prayers in the best possible way.

THINGS THEY SAY

"Sometimes I'm tempted to doubt the 'universal' aspect of Jesus, especially when some say that He wasn't unique."

* * *

The Answer:

"There is only Christ . . . He is everything, and He is in everything."

"*All* things were made by Him."

"Jesus Christ is the same yesterday, today and for ever."

* * *

Jesus says:

"I am the Light of the world."

* * *

THINGS THEY SAY.

"Not even those dearest to me seem really to understand my deep longings."

*   *   *

"He will keep in perfect peace those who trust in Him."

"*The Lord* will be your everlasting light. . . . Your sun shall never set!"

"True wisdom is God's . . . He *understands* . . . His understanding is unlimited."

*   *   *

THINGS THEY SAY

"After what life has done to me, I seem to have no fight left in me."

*   *   *

The Answer:

"We have the Lord our God to fight our battles for us!"

"He gives power to the worn-out, and strength to the weak. . . . They that wait upon the Lord shall renew their strength."

*   *   *

The risen Jesus says:

"My power will show up best in your weakness!"

*   *   *

22

Dynamic Patience

I once had a rather alarming experience as a passenger in a car driven by the head of an international manufacturing concern. . . .

"I'm afraid I'm not a very patient person", said my friend. Then, as if to prove his point, he left the road whenever a queue of traffic threatened to slow him down. Onto the grass verges or into the nearest lay-by he would go, overtaking the queue, and boldly rejoining the road ahead of the others. Ignoring all angry looks. . . .

I began to see the secret of my friend's business success . . . but felt very relieved to arrive safely at our destination!

*　*　*

Bridging The Gap

Genuine patience is a rather rare gift these days . . . even among Christians. Perhaps some of us are getting a little impatient, now, about the working-out of some of those promises. . . ?

What is it that helps us to wait composedly for some of

God's blessings? What fills the "vacuum" while we're waiting?

Most of us experience times when expectations (including our spiritual ones) seem unreal, God's promises postponed indefinitely. All that stubbornly remains, somewhere deep inside, is the thought, "At least, I know that He loves me".

I've found that the vacuum starts to be filled once we realize what a lot of promise-realization is contained in just the loving *presence* of Jesus. It's at vacuum-times, times of temptation to be discouraged, when that one thing of which we do feel sure – His love – can, in a remarkable way, help us to feel that delays don't matter quite so much.

In the midst of our disappointments we give a trusting look into that love, as if to say, "All right, Lord . . . Your love will do for the moment. I'll go on waiting for the things You've promised." We accept the wait more easily, knowing that His love guarantees the eventual arrival of what has been promised.

A very useful skill for a Christian to acquire is learning to "feed upon" God's sheer love before the full realization of some of the soul-satisfactions for which we've been waiting. I've found that when I can, so to speak, picture the love of Jesus beaming down on me (good to make this frequent if we can!), my impatience to see circumstances change starts to disappear.

At any given moment that love-sense can help us to feel that *everything* promised to God's followers will eventually be ours.

*   *   *

Content With Him

It is God's love which provides the *continuity* of our promise-journey. From time to time God's blessings come to us . . . as if, in some way, a partial realization of what is planned for us. Between those high points, however, there need be no vacuum, no discouragement.

When there's "nothing much happening" in the spiritual-blessing area, we can simply look up into that love, and need no argument that the Lord really is at work and that whatever comes will be perfectly timed. We'll even accept, fairly happily, that some promises haven't worked out exactly as we imagined God intended for us!

Yes, the more "lost" we become in Jesus's love the more sure we'll be about what He has promised to us.

All spiritual desires are well worth developing, of course. We would be strange Christians if we didn't look forward to an existence free from physical and mental pain, where the happiness we wish for people we know who have suffered much, will come at last.

The important thing is that the desire for those things promised to us must never become stronger than the desire for *Him*. There's so much to be brought into harmony on the way to those promised rewards, but if we can enjoy *now* the amazing gift of Jesus Himself, it will help to disperse our spiritual impatience.

Here's the remarkable thing for promise-followers. . .' As soon as we surrender to the warmth of Jesus's love we begin to experience, *in the present*, much of what is contained in the promises. His love does so much for us that we are content to wait for those blissful earth-free states

* * *

Dynamic Patience
Not Just Passivity

As we allow ourselves to "exist" in Jesus's love, something inside tells us that whatever He has in store for us must be exactly right. His scheme, as affecting the details of our life (here, and in a future existence), can safely be left with Him.

And so, we are wise to spend a lot of time consciously letting that love beam on us, letting ourselves absorb it. . . . This won't only give us patience, but will set free our spirits. We'll find that our spirits are able to disentangle themselves from many of the limiting factors which would hold up our enjoyment of love's highest gifts.

The great secret to be learned by a follower of Jesus, therefore, is to allow His always available love-influence to bring us something of those promises *now*.

On our way to the full possession of what God has promised, a foretaste of what is to come can be experienced even in the most discouraging settings. As long as His love is there! As we prepare the conditions (by setting aside a little time, by our sheer trust and by our "enthusiasm" about Jesus) for experiencing His love, we will gain a stronger-than-ever confidence in those wonderful promises.

There are two things which can't be separated: (1) Jesus's love, and (2) a sense that His promises won't fail. This is why that patient "receiving" of His love is no mere passivity, no waiting for our share of pie-in-the-sky. The patience we manage to show in His love is dynamic . . . it's making sure that those promises won't be held up for a day longer than necessary.

Sometimes people feel that it is our patience which slows things down. Within God's scheme, it's our patience which may even be hurrying things along a little!

PROMISE FOR TODAY

"Keep within My love . . . and your cup of joy will overflow."

GRASPING THE PROMISE

Dear Lord, please let me make it an instinct, when things are not working out as I had hoped, to feed upon Your love.

I will let the influence of that love give me that much needed patience on my journey towards Your promises.

I most certainly believe Your promise, here, of joy for those who will keep Your love in the foreground. I make that promise mine now.

DAILY REMINDER NO. 20

Lord Jesus, thank You for Your love – within me and around me – bringing me patience in the complexities of today.

THINGS THEY SAY

"I find decisions so difficult. Either choice seems surrounded by fear."

* * *

The Answer:

"If you *really* want to do what God wants you to do, remember that He is ready to give you a generous supply of wisdom."

"All things work together for good for those who love and trust God."

* * *

Jesus says:

"You *shall* know the truth, and the truth shall set you free.

* * *

THINGS THEY SAY

"Am I fooling myself in hoping for better things one day?"

*   *   *

The Answer:

"God has always promised a crown of life to those who trust in Him!"

"It is God who called you to share in the life of our Lord Jesus . . . and God keeps faith."

"If we are faithful to the end, trusting God, we will share in all that belongs to Christ."

"He is the God who keeps every promise."

*   *   *

THINGS THEY SAY

"Is God *really* aware of my need. . . ? Will His help soon come?"

* * *

The Answer:

"You can be strong and without fear because your God is coming to save you."

"The Lord is not too weak to save you."

* * *

God says:

"Even before you call on Me, I am answering you."

* * *

23

Love's Continuity

The barrier between our life on this planet and that which awaits us in another dimension doesn't really exist . . . at least not in God's eyes.

It is helpful if we can really grasp this idea, and see God's *love*, always, as the vital link . . . fulfilling promises for us now, and fulfilling them in the future – all part of one uninterrupted process.

*   *   *

Promises Already Kept

As God's plans for His creation unfold, those who have taken hold of some of His promises can begin to see both the present and the future significance of those promises. Looking around us (and also catching just the odd glance, perhaps, of our spiritual progress!) we may find ourselves saying, "Hey! That's just what God promised me". This *recognition* will then fill us with even greater certainty about the things which are to come.

The love surrounding us now is, of course, the same

as that which will surround us after our present bodies have worn out. "Love will outlast everything", said Paul.

As we mentioned earlier, love links our spiritual present with our spiritual future. Not only that, but it's our guarantee that there will be a future! Peter wrote: "The new life which you now have will last for ever, because it comes from Jesus Christ."

Most of those who really trust God's promises will try (with varying degrees of determination) to keep close to Him throughout each day. As we keep as close as possible, we begin to see a little of the working-out, within the circumstances in which we're set, of God's long-term intention for us. If His love is not far from our thoughts, we shall have an increasing recognition of this process. "You've become part of Him and therefore share His new life. One day you will rise . . . as He did", promised Paul.

Keeping God within reach, so to speak, we'll notice many things which have an "air" of promise about them . . . a sense that they are part of a *developing process*. This is why it's such a good habit to thank God for each gain we make, however small, each threatening situation which He prevented from getting worse (usually many within a day).

We should be especially grateful, for these are promises kept, in the here and now. And there's a continuity sense . . . that more promise-realization is on the way.

* * *

Grateful Detection

God doesn't want us to miss the vital significance of each step of progress, each conquest of the old self . . . these are times of real thankfulness because they're *leading us forward* to that soul-perfection which He has promised us.

When we thank God for the fact of His promises and for the hope which they inject into our often tough existence, we can thank Him, too, that the quality of our life *now* is being enriched by them. We can thank Him for the changes which our acceptance of those promises are creating *now*.

Joy may not come too easily for some of us; it can seem an almost cruel word to many struggling Christians, can't it? But a little quiet rejoicing does become possible as we train ourselves to look carefully for some of the things promised by God being actualized in our present circumstances. Sometimes these things may seem hard to find but they're worth watching out for – eagerly. We shall not usually be disappointed. The usual temptation is to notice the failures – and to fail to see the blessings – and the improvements!

As we start to detect those little blessings and "gains", it dawns on us that some of the promises have come out from the category of cautious hope into the category of actualization. It dawns on us that the promises are a *verifiable influence* on our present circumstances.

All those little spiritual insights which we acquire now are widening out for us into that pure and undistorted "view" of Jesus our Lord which is our promised destiny. "Some day we're going to see Him in His completeness – face to face", said Paul.

Promise-Building

With each little victory in withstanding evil's subtle pressures, with each occasion of God getting His way, we move forward towards the time when those dark forces will leave us completely unmoved.

Here's Peter again: "As you know Jesus better, He will give you, through His great power, everything you need for living an utterly good life. . . . By that same power, He gives us all the rich and wonderful blessings which He has promised."

Each occasion of love and sacrifice (even though we may feel that they have a "self"-motivation at times), is a stage in a continuing process. This process is gradually shaping our life to be like that of Jesus Himself. One of the similarities will be a growing capacity to care deeply, as He does, for His children.

Each "encounter" with Jesus, however brief, each priceless few moments of feeling absolutely sure of His love, are further examples of promise-continuity. Building up for us is that *sure* knowledge . . . that awareness of Him which will be uninterrupted. "Your reward", wrote Peter, "will be a never-ending share in Christ's glory and honour." Thank you, Peter!

So let's start really to value every little detail we notice of God's activity, every little danger averted, every little ethical gain. Don't let's despise even the smallest of these things, and certainly don't willingly surrender any progress made.

Valuing these things as we go along the promise-road with Jesus, means that we'll start to see their unmistakable eternal significance.

PROMISES FOR TODAY

Jesus says:

"I am the Beginning and the End."

"Happy are those whose hearts are pure, for they will see God."

GRASPING THE PROMISES

Lord Jesus, I realize that only the road travelled with You leads anywhere at all! Help me to allow Your good influence all the time, so that I can progress towards purity of heart, and one day see You.

Help me to notice how Your promises are beginning to work out in my life. I firmly grasp *all* Your promises about the future of those who follow You. Thank You.

DAILY REMINDER NO. 21

Lord, thank You that You are constantly at work today . . . shaping my present – and my future!

24

Realists . . . But Optimists!

Many people wonder, no doubt complacently, what it will be like when they step into heaven. Some can imagine themselves coming into the Lord's presence and hearing a slightly stern, but affectionate, "Well, now. . . ."

For once, I'm sure that even clergy and ministers will be lost for words!

Anyway, there He'll be . . . beyond all argument. It will dawn on us, I'm certain, that He has been looking forward eagerly to our meeting . . . even more than we have.

For a long time He has been getting things ready for us.

We could have been depriving ourselves of pleasurably anticipating all this by not grasping those promises (at least, until we read this book!) On the other hand, if we have wholeheartedly made the promises ours, we could be excused from thinking that we had had one foot in heaven already. . . .

* * *

Still More Plans

One obvious result of having lived by God's promises is finding that the spirit-realm won't be a completely new environment. Rather than being carried away by the things which the world pursues so fiercely, we will have been enjoying something of that heavenly climate instead.

If those promises have become part of us, God will be able to take us by the hand and gently introduce us to an even greater awareness of how much He loves us, and of what wonderful plans He still has for us. The promises will melt into a marvellous sense of our really being at home in our new environment.

God will have such a lot to show us! Those puzzling things about our existence here will now have the light of truth on them – a light which was partially hidden by the blind alleys and distortions of the earthly scene.

Don't you feel that when we arrive at that fully realized "possession" of Jesus our Lord, we won't be restlessly longing for more? . . . Except that many others might share this with us!

Even in that eventual place of promise-realization we know that there will still be a *looking forward*. We'll be aware that God's purposes of love are ongoing. We'll long to see increasing numbers (still trying to make something of life in this earth's context) being drawn into God.

Our original decision to trust God's promises was made in the anything-but-favourable conditions of the late twentieth century. In order to cope with those conditions, and not to let go the promises, we will have had to develop many soul qualities . . . notably a genuine trust. Obviously, God will have to develop further those qualities and eliminate those impurities in us.

No matter how long we may have left on the earth, a wonderful opportunity now exists for us to bring the atmosphere of the promises into the most humdrum, the most discouraging places. The influence of the promise-Maker will follow promise-recipients wherever they go!

* * *

Stabilizing

Have we *joyfully* accepted the promises? Have we let them *immediately* affect our life?

If so, we are going to sense a warmth of approval from God as our life becomes more and more consistent with those promises, and as we start (at last!) to take Him at His word. We'll be learning now what *love* is all about . . . both in its giving and in its receiving sense.

The promise-based life is, above everything else, a love-based life. The "details" on the promise-journey won't matter as much as they used to, because love is carrying us forward. And we're going to find glimpses of God in all sorts of places. . . .

"Hope" can sound a slightly pathetic word to the sceptical person. For the promise-follower, however, the word doesn't seem quite adequate to describe what is much more of an inner certainty about the basic security of existence in God's care.

Like others, a promise-recipient won't know everything which tomorrow is going to produce . . . but he or she will be able to see through what may be tomorrow's fluctuations, its fussy or hurtful details.

171

Even if we're only in the early stages of relying on the promises, we'll find that they have become a tremendous *stabilizing influence*. We become steadier persons, as we depend less upon feelings, and more upon God's unchangeability. As we said earlier, those promises will be helping us to see our short life here in its true perspective. If we have staked everything upon the promises, I'm sure we'll find that they are precisely what we're going to receive . . . nothing less!

So let's really enjoy the thought that so much is being lovingly got ready for us . . . and that God's Spirit is ready to work overtime in us to see that we don't mess it all up!

*   *   *

The Difference

For as long as God goes on loving us, so will that love's expression, in a process of blessing His children, continue. In other words, those promises *must* work out.

It's worth recalling, frequently, that God's promises are indivisible from our relationship with Him . . . not statements which we can either graciously "accept" or set aside.

Just watch how the trust-content of prayers is now increased by the encouragement of those promises, how the atmosphere of heaven is brought into this world's existence.

It is important to recognize the difference between mere wishful thinking and the optimism which accompanies acceptance of God's promises. Mere wishful thinking never stands up to those uncomfortable moments of truth perception. We feel an uneasiness about persisting in our wishful thinking; we feel that we're deceiving ourselves with comforting thoughts. . . .

But the conviction about the future which the promises produce inside us is something entirely different. . . . We recognize that there's no element of conflict, no misgivings, about that wonderful hope which has emerged.

When we indulge in wishful thinking, the "realistic" self keeps breaking in and labelling our hope as suspect. When we're following God's promises, however, there's no such suspicion . . . in fact we feel that the promises deserve even more joy, even more eager anticipation from us.

* * *

Convinced

We must firmly close the door now on all thoughts, inspired by evil, that our looking-forward has misplaced; we must firmly close the door, also, on thoughts that we'd better soak up all that this world can offer, because it's all that there is.

With that sense of the continuing love of Jesus, we can quietly "look around" our life, and begin to see evidence of His promise-keeping. What a neglected exercise this is among Christians! We can begin to see the Divine anticipation in coming to our help in a variety of ways. The increasingly sure results of living by those promises, the sense of what is ours, will naturally cause us to thank the Lord, perhaps many times in a day.

Yes, there are *so many* things promised to the followers of Jesus, as He acts as our world's light. Our recognition of His present promise-keeping will leave us more and more convinced about all that is on its way. Whenever we think of that Divine love, let's not forget all that is coming to us as an expression of that love . . .

It will be a revolutionary feeling for many of us that we needn't be afraid, now, to reach out to others . . . confident in the promised strength being there, rather than hoping that God might "move" to strengthen us a little.

If God's promises have now got into us, affecting our daily living, we'll have that future-sense which completes the resources of any believer. This future-sense, as we said earlier, brings genuine peace, and gives us a marvellous patience, as we work our way through life's uncertainties.

*　　*　　*

Harmony

As we have seen, the whole process of living by God's promises is essentially a *receiving* one. In the early stages we "receive" serenity and a wonderful sense of anticipation. And later . . . well! Eventually, I'm sure that we'll be overwhelmed by the full realization of those promises. "Children of promise", certain that God's love won't fail them, find every aspect of living brought into harmony with this basic certainty. . . .

True promise-followers *want* to be, and *want* to do, only what is consistent with the sphere dominated by the presence of Jesus our Lord (even if not always succeeding!) They increasingly see the results of following those promises by progress made in areas where there used to be frequent failures. Where there used to be misgivings, for example, there's now a serene contemplation of that divine reliability.

The things about which Jesus spoke, such as "the Kingdom of God" and "Eternal Life", are really all about knowing God. This is why getting better acquainted with God through joyfully accepting His promises means that the phrase "Thy Kingdom come" (often said mechanically) now starts to mean something.

* * *

In case all those hopeful things we've quoted from Bible authors seem to ignore one or two facts, it's worth remembering that those who expressed such wonderful things were realists . . . immersed in a world of poverty, cruelty, and premature death. These people were just the sort to conclude, sadly, that life was a bad joke with no purpose, nothing to look forward to.

But, instead, God's promises had hit these people squarely between the eyes. All at once (especially when Jesus came), they became "crazy" optimists, in addition to being realists.

It's as though those New Testament writers (now enjoying the promises!) are looking longingly in our direction and saying: "Now, look. You can't go wrong if you gamble on what *we* wrote."

* * *

Here's just a small and familiar extract from among the countless "hopeful" passages. We could do worse than to take a little look at this picture every day:

> There was a vast crowd . . . including people who had known great suffering. . . .
>
> But they were now praising God!
>
> Here's God actually living among His people, wiping away all their tears. . . .
>
> Pain and sorrow are things of the past.
>
> These people don't need the sun or bright lamps . . . *God* is their light.
>
> And the One on the throne is telling us: "I am making everything new."

If each person who has pinned his or her hopes on Jesus can *also* make sure that those Divine promises now burn brightly inside them, the phrase "struggling Christians" is going to disappear!